" … Practicing these helpful tips will strengthen your ability to effectively meet stress when it happens and find the proper resources you need to help you on your journey … easy to read, well written, and filled with practical and useful advice … I strongly recommend Dr. Kendra Lowe's book for military spouses, as well as for law enforcement spouses, and their family members."

—Christi Luby, PhD, MPH, MCHES®, CFE

"All DoD military and civilian senior leaders should include *Milspouse Strength* on their recommended reading lists … Dr. Lowe not only acknowledges the unique challenges we face as military spouses, but she provides the tools we need to navigate what can often be a stressful way of life … There is no doubt her book will make a difference for years to come."

—Leslie Janaros, US Air Force brat, veteran, and military spouse

"Truly outstanding! … Kendra captures the true essence of being a military spouse, the challenges, the resilience, the stress and the rewards … "

—Robyn Grable, US Navy veteran and military spouse; CEO, Veterans ASCEND

"This is the ultimate must-have guide for all military spouses … a step-by-step guide that will enable spouses to build their individual skills, give them the ability to reduce their stress levels, and improve their emotional and mental wellbeing … comprehensive, concise and beautifully constructed, it can be read as a whole or used as a quick reference guide … "

—Debbie Laaff, NATO resiliency trainer, international military spouse

" … so many stories … resonated with me … reminded me that it's not about ignoring the stresses or being 'strong enough' to not succumb to the impacts of stress; it's about designing new strategies rooted in personal honesty that carry you through the valley … This isn't a 'take a self-care day, you'll feel better' book. It's a 'hey, this life can be hard and not all stresses are the same … find new ways to recognize the nuances and emerge stronger on the other side' … "

—Jen Pasquale, founder, Pride & Grit

" … clinically and medically sound while being easy for a reader to follow along step by step. As a civilian clinical psychologist working for military families, what Dr. Lowe writes resonated … I'm so eager to share this book with families."

—Dr. Mariah Coe, PhD, CPhT, EDIS, Naval Health Clinic, Bahrain

" … gracefully leads you through steps to understand what stress is, understand that stress comes in many forms and many levels, and then guides you through steps and processes to learn to handle stressful situations … The tools and tips given throughout the book will leave you stronger and better able to handle all the stress that this crazy and wonderful military life throws your way … "

—Suzie Schwartz, proud Air Force spouse

"Dr. Lowe does a wonderful job of explaining the stress cycle in a way that is relevant and relatable. She identifies common stressors that many military spouses experience throughout their member's career. She uses evidence-based actionable strategies that are grounded in research and best practice to help military spouses break out of the stress cycle ... "

—Marinelle Reynolds, MSW, LCSW

" ... Dr. Lowe does an outstanding job describing and explaining how to identify stress and how to work through it ... This book opened my eyes to a reality that so many of us experience, but somehow we put it under the rug instead of facing it and working through it ... This book will not only help you see clearly but it will teach you some wonderful techniques."

— Verenice Castillo, CEO, Military Spouse Advocacy Network

" ... a poignant, insightful approach to the challenges faced by military spouses ... Dr. Lowe's many relatable examples and her engaging writing style draw the reader in as she offers simple, practical ideas to help readers manage stress and carve a positive path as individuals and in their role in a military family."

—Kathy Roth-Douquet, CEO, Blue Star Families

"I laughed and cried while reading this amazing book! What a wake-up call! Being proactive about stress management can catch you at the bottom of the roller-coaster. I really like the reflection sections throughout the book as they make you stop and really think about Kendra's messages. I love the stories shared in each section and the practical advice, resources, and tools provided."

—Elizabeth Castro, 2019, 2020, 2021 AFI Camp Courtney Military Spouse of the Year

"Military life is a beautiful tapestry of heroic moments and immense hardships. Balanced mental, emotional, and spiritual health are critical for our military families ... to handle the whirlwind lifestyle ... and operation tempo that is critical to mission success. *Milspouse Strength* provides valuable skills, insights, and purposeful direction to help new and seasoned military spouses navigate the elevated stressors that only military families can understand ... "

—Kerri Jeter, Army veteran and spouse; founder, Freedom Sisters Media

" ... a must read for every military spouse! ... keen insight into the challenges of military life ... a plethora of user-friendly tips ... The reader will come away with insights and tools to thrive as a milspouse."

—Janet Kerr, MA, LPC

" ... So often we are called upon to step into roles with little to no warning or training, and by using this book a milspouse would be able to set themselves (and others) up for a positive and successful experience. Milspouses, this book is for us and written by one of our own. It is impossible not to find yourself described in one of the stories or examples."

—Brenna Van Stone, Air Force key spouse, milspouse employment networking specialist

Milspouse Strength

~~~~~~~~~~~~~~~~~~~~~~~

Changing the Way You See and Respond to Military Life Stress

~~~~~~~~~~~~~~~~~~~~~~~

Kendra Lowe

MSc, EdS, EdD, NCSP, LSSP

Elva Resa ∗ Saint Paul

Milspouse Strength:
Changing the Way You See and Respond to Military Life Stress
©2022 by Kendra Lowe

The information and advice presented by the author is intended to encourage military families. Each situation is unique, and individuals should seek professional or medical support as appropriate.

Design by Andermax Studios.

Library of Congress Control Number: 2021948352

ISBN: 978-1-934617-63-2 (pb)
978-1-934617-68-7 (epub)

Printed in the United States of America.
1S 2 3 4 5

Elva Resa Publishing
8362 Tamarack Vlg Ste 119-106
St Paul, MN 55125
ElvaResa.com
MilitaryFamilyBooks.com

To my husband and three children.
You make the impossible possible.

Contents

~~~~~~~~~~~~~~~~~~~~~~~~

Introduction

~~~~~~~~~~~~~~~~~~~~~~~~~~~~~~~

SIX MONTHS INTO OUR NEW ASSIGNMENT in Okinawa, Japan, my husband finally sat me down and pleaded for me to "get my head in the game." He knew I was still struggling to accept the news we had received our first night on the island: our two-year tour would actually be four years, shifting our "adventure" into what seemed like a lifetime to me. The additional stress of the recent loss of my grandfather with no option to travel back for his funeral compounded the stresses of unemployment, prolonged single-parent duties due to my husband's training, and distance from familial support systems. I felt overwhelmed and alone. My husband's plea forced me to accept that my usual coping skills—exercising and journaling—weren't working.

As I sat down that night to devise a plan, I stumbled across an email for wall decor words. One phrase stood out to me right away: **Wake Up, Kick Ass, Repeat**. I immediately ordered it in the largest, darkest letters possible and adhered it to our wall, where it remained for the four years. Initially it served as a reminder and daily challenge, but I soon discovered that adding this mantra to the wall gave me the strength to shift my negative thoughts to positive ones. As additional challenges arose during that assignment—the loss of my two remaining grandparents, high-risk missions my husband endured, more unemployment and underemployment, and prolonged isolation—I approached and responded to the stress in a more positive and meaningful way. The mental shift significantly improved both my personal and familial strength.

As I started to share my experience with other military spouses, there was an instant connection. Military spouses began approaching me after talks with visible relief in their eyes, telling me how alone they had previously felt in their struggles. For me, and for these spouses, relief accompanied hope. Hope that we could take action to improve our own social and emotional health. Hope that we could begin to enjoy life again and break the endless cycle of stress, sadness, and exhaustion.

I wrote this book to help more military spouses find relief and hope by practicing techniques that help them handle the significant stress built into military life. Working through this resource will help you understand the complex nature of stress and cope with the perpetual challenges of being a military spouse. You will reflect on the potential challenges you may face, self-assess the significance of stress, and have a better game plan for each situation that comes your way. I encourage you to write in a journal to capture your thoughts and reflections as you read the book.

Approaching stress differently makes a difference, as shown by a message I received from one military spouse:

> *"I recently finished working through your material with six military spouses through virtual meetings and want to let you know the positive change we have all experienced. We are now more accepting of others' stress, we know we are not alone, and your tools allowed us to take control of our mental health."*

Something has called you here to begin this journey—a significant setback, a desire to learn, or possibly a deeper awareness that you are not alone. Doing so requires vulnerability by leaving behind the old and being open to the new. Know that you are not the person you were five years ago, and you have a choice in who you will be five years from now. Through this journey, you will be better prepared for future challenges by daring yourself to open your eyes and see stress through a different lens, a lens that will ultimately serve as your daily mantra to hurdle barriers, recover faster, and become stronger.

CHAPTER 1

Understand

Calm the Chaos

*What's going on outside does not always match
what's going on inside.*

LATE ON A FRIDAY AFTERNOON I finished signing my separation papers and hung up my uniform for the last time—believing it to be a seamless transition. I recall the excitement to support my husband as he continued to serve and I entered a new world of possibilities. I had been a military spouse for the past six years while serving on active duty, and I naively assumed this transition would be like the others. I failed to account for the unseen privileges that come from wearing a uniform at the same time: established jobs, resources, colleagues, and purpose. I lacked the tools to identify and minimize the unique stress associated with my new role as a military spouse. I blindly walked the path, stumbling far too many times to count, trying to wrap my head around my distorted view of "stress." A mere month into the transition, I felt overwhelmed.

I quickly learned that military spouses, brand new or seasoned, experience stress and military life together. Though stress is a seemingly simple word, it has unique meaning for military life. Military life compounds common life stressors for military spouses and creates complex challenges like financial struggles, isolation from friends and family, and lengthy periods away from their service member. Military families have repeated transitions and lifestyle changes that make it difficult to assess and cope with stress.

These often-hidden layers of stress continue to build up, especially when they are unexpected. It might be the feeling of grief as you say goodbye at the start of a deployment. Sometimes it is loneliness or feeling lost in a new community where you have yet to find friends to provide support through the deployment. If you are reading this book, then you have undoubtedly spent time and energy thinking about the stress associated with military life. Learning about the nature of stress and how to minimize its effects will help you navigate this stress now and in the future.

Unfortunately, military spouses can become trapped in an ineffective and counterproductive cycle of negative thoughts and feelings. Commonly recognized as a "negative stress loop," this cycle consists of a stressful event, negative reaction, physical and emotional wear and tear, and reduced health from poor management of the stress. As the cycle repeats, it weakens your system and increases sensitivity to future stress. It can feel like a social and emotional rollercoaster.

Rickety Rollercoaster

"I feel like I am on this endless, rickety rollercoaster. I deliberately chug up the tracks to the top, and I sit there waiting for the fall—because I know it is coming. I just don't know when it is going to be, where it is going to be, and what it is going to be yet. Then it hits; my husband gets tasked with a 365-day tour in Afghanistan. I plummet to the bottom with that sickening feeling in my stomach, afraid that I won't be caught at the bottom— afraid that the bottom is too vast and too deep. But I find the bottom, and I am raw. Military spouses reach out to help, but there is nothing to do to help because the fact is you can't change the situation. So I climb inside myself and wait for it to get better. Sometimes it takes weeks or months, and I lose a little of myself each time. But I know I'm capable of being happy again because I've been there before, at the top of the ride. It just gets harder as time goes on to chug up the tracks, and I can't help but think there must be a better way for me to do this." —A., Army spouse

It is easy to feel trapped by stress, but this feeling doesn't have to be permanent. You can work yourself out of this negative stress loop by adopting a new cycle of stress growth. Stress growth involves recognizing and anticipating stress before reacting to it, by developing a deeper understanding of the word stress and assessing your own stress triggers. The cycle's final challenge is critical self-analysis that strengthens your preparedness for future stress. Challenging situations then become prime opportunities to grow and thrive rather than potential pitfalls with long-lasting negative effects.

Stress growth involves recognizing and anticipating stress before reacting to it, by developing a deeper understanding of the word stress and assessing your own stress triggers.

So how do you achieve this? How can you begin this new cycle to better understand the complex nature of stress? How can you better see the positive effects of your growth? The answers to these questions may mean survival for military spouses. But that's why you're here. You're determined to take back control of your life, to free yourself from the constant cycle of negative stress. Before we can break the stress cycle, we need to understand what stress is, where it comes from, and how it affects us.

Definition of Stress

Stress is certainly not a new concept. Researchers have studied it for years, searching for answers and hoping to find a common denominator so stress can be better treated. But stress factors are elusive and there is not a one-size-fits-all approach. In simplest terms, stress is the amount you feel overwhelmed or unable to cope as a result of an experience. Unfortunately, this straightforward definition does not consider all the other significant components of stress. For example, stress can be caused externally by your environment or internally by your thoughts. There are also varying degrees of stress that can have mild or severe effects on your social and emotional well-being. Going even deeper, stress is not always bad for you and can sometimes be an extremely rewarding experience.

One of the most difficult aspects of stress is that you often can't see it or its impact while you're "in it." My epiphany regarding being blinded while "in it" came after the loss of my niece. I had just finished my 5 a.m. CrossFit workout and I was preparing an egg omelet when my cell phone rang. It was odd that my mother was calling so early in the morning, so I immediately stopped and answered the phone. I could barely make out what she was saying between sobs, but my brain kicked in and put the pieces together. My sister had gone into labor that night. Per protocol, when she arrived at the hospital the nurse hooked her up to IVs and monitors and then checked for the baby's heartbeat. Nothing. The baby's umbilical cord had wrapped around her neck during early labor, and my sister had to deliver a child who had already passed away.

Stress can be caused externally by your environment or internally by your thoughts.

My husband was on temporary duty travel (TDY) and out of cell phone contact; I knew I would have to brave this alone. I moved through the next week in a task-oriented state as I met with the priest, picked scripture readings and flowers, and prepared the eulogy my sister asked me to give at the funeral. Knowing the last job was the most significant, I avoided lengthy conversations with friends and family members at the church and tried to avert my eyes as I watched four grown men carry the tiniest casket up the aisle. I knew my sister needed me to be strong, so I let my brain dictate actions that blocked my heart.

Days later I was able to take a breath and talk with my husband. I started to fill him in, talking a mile a minute. Finally, he stopped me and asked the question I had avoided to that point: "How are YOU doing?" My brain relinquished control to my heart. Until then I couldn't, nor did I want to, see just how much this tragic event had affected me.

Being able to step outside your own situation as an observer creates a more unbiased lens through which you see stress. This lens unfolds the layers of your life, including those you don't necessarily associate with military life, and helps you understand and self-assess the impact of stress.

Nature of Stress

Stressful events can become blurred over time. They begin to look and feel the same, and you find yourself thinking: "It's all just stress." But lumping stress together into one basket prevents us from seeing which stressful events are within our control and which are not.

Stressful events can be imposed on us or by us—and that's an important distinction. Internal stress includes uncomfortable thoughts, feelings, or expectations. Thinking you will never find close friends in your new community, feeling apprehensive about the return of your spouse from a lengthy deployment, or expecting your mother to call and check in on you once a week are examples. These stressors come from within.

External stressors are events that happen to you or around you. Major life changes such as marriage, pregnancy, or unpredictable moves (maybe even all at once) are common examples. Even small environmental factors can be stressful, such as a neighbor's barking dog, the sudden cry of a child, the frigid cold of Montana, or the suffering heat of Texas. As military spouses, the list of external stressors is often quite long.

There are also situations where both types of stress are present. All too often, our response to external stress becomes internal. An unexpected deployment may drive thoughts of fear and worry. It is important to understand how both types of stress impact your well-being, since most internal stress is within your control and most external stress is not. For military spouses this distinction is profound, as we are required to function in external circumstances with very little control. Take comfort in knowing there are things you can change.

> **Reflect:** Start to open your lens by separating external and internal stress. In your journal, describe your most recent stressor and evaluate whether it was internal (thoughts, feelings, behaviors, expectations), external (major life change, environment, unpredictable event), or a combination of both.

Severity of Stress

Not all stress is created equal. It is easier to recover from a broken dishwasher than a move to a foreign country. Understanding how to measure the severity of stress is another key skill to help you gauge its impact on your well-being.

Stress can be measured in three different ways: frequency, duration, and intensity.

Frequency

The frequency of the event, or how often it occurs, can greatly impact stress levels. An event with less frequency could be a disagreement with housing when they told you base housing was full, harsh feedback from your boss that you were not expecting, or frustration over the dog magically escaping the fence. It happens, but it isn't a regular occurrence.

High-frequency events continually happen. For example, your teenage daughter picks daily fights with you about her clothes, or you fear for your deployed spouse's safety. It is a consistent part of each day that escalates your stress levels.

Frequency Scale

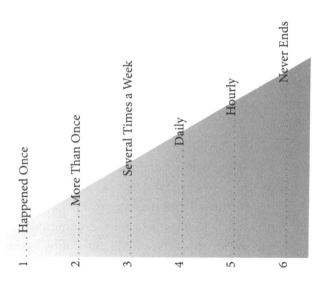

Duration

Stress can also be measured by duration, or how long a stressful event occurs. A flat tire on your way to work or a fleeting doubt that your friend will follow through with your exercise date does not last long. Conversely, a global pandemic, a parent's battle with cancer, or feelings of sadness that you do not live close to your family are stressors that span greater time. These events often do not have a concrete end and can heighten stress levels.

Duration Scale

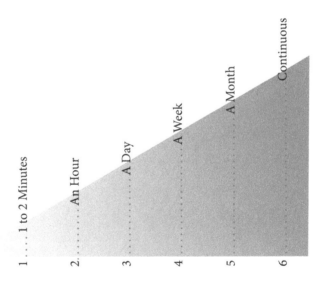

Intensity

Probably the hardest to discern and most significant of the three measurements is intensity. Intensity is like the pain scale you see in your doctor's office—the one with the green happy face to the left and red pained face to the right with descending happy faces in between. You are expected to pick the face that best matches your current level of pain. Basically, intensity is how much you feel it.

Unlike frequency and duration where it is easier to identify the number of occurrences and time, intensity is purely subjective and unique to you. One military spouse may be thrilled about moving to Florida because it will be the first time they will be within driving distance of their parents. Although moving is still stressful for this spouse, it is less intense because of the way they perceive the experience. Another military spouse moving to the same location may be leaving a location they have grown to love. They feel this move more intensely because they perceive it as a loss. It is important to remember that the intensity of a stressful situation is personal, not to be compared to others. If it is intense for you, then it is real.

Intensity Scale

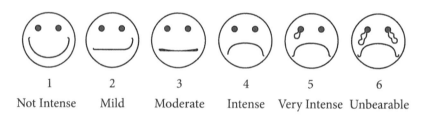

| 1 | 2 | 3 | 4 | 5 | 6 |
| Not Intense | Mild | Moderate | Intense | Very Intense | Unbearable |

> **Reflect:** Revisit the stressful event you wrote about. Note where it falls on the intensity scale.

Now that you have identified where your stress originates and how it measures in frequency, duration, and intensity, the next step is to analyze the cumulative effect of all three together. If you only measure your stress individually in each category, you miss the dynamic interaction they have with each other. This interaction is called the stress's severity and can be measured as mild, moderate, or critical.

The severity of stress depends on how the three measurements interact. For example, your car breaks down on the way to work (external). In one scenario, the car breaking down could be a moderate stress level (intensity), occurring once (frequency), and lasting an hour (duration). This would place the stressful event at a moderate level of severity.

Now change the situation slightly. Perhaps your spouse has been deployed for three months (external), you are feeling anxious that morning because you're running late for an important meeting at work (internal anxiety), and then your car breaks down (external). In this scenario, the accumulating stress shifted the intensity from moderate to unbearable. The event still only occurred once (frequency) and lasted an hour (duration), but the intensity of the stress increased the overall severity to critical. When stress compounds, it increases the severity.

A recent experience regarding compounding stress occurred after our move to Texas. I had stepped outside that morning and started a slow jog, telling myself as I did most mornings: "You'll feel better after a few miles." I was tired since I hadn't sleep well the night before. My mind was racing with thoughts of my children's adjustment to their new home, starting a new job, how many boxes I had left to unpack, finding a veterinarian for the dog, getting my driver's license renewed, missing friends, and well, pretty much all things associated with a move back to the States after being overseas for four years.

I blared my music louder to drown out my thoughts and allow the lyrics to motivate me up endless hills. As I finished the last mile and walked up to the house, I saw my oldest daughter standing outside, all geared up in black leggings and running shoes. She asked if I would mind going around the block a few times with her. I immediately thought of my endless to-do list and wanted to postpone, but I saw the eagerness in her face and knew I couldn't say no.

I put the headphones down in the garage and started out again, this time with a chatty nine-year-old. She told me ideas for her new room. "Purple, I really want my room to be bright purple. You know it's my favorite color. Maybe a reading spot with lights. We could transform my closet into a secret place?" Paint, curtains, ordering lights all added to the list in my head. I nodded and told her they were all great options. She reminded me how we couldn't paint in our last house on base. We talked about our old house and laughed about how many times the toilet overflowed due to old plumbing.

Then she got quiet. I didn't think much of it. We often focused on breathing while running, and I assumed she was doing just that. Until she abruptly stopped next to me and bent over crying. I immediately asked if she was okay, and she could barely respond between sobs. "Thinking of Okinawa reminds me of my friends. I miss my friends. I miss them so much it hurts. What if I can't make friends here? What if they don't like me?"

My stomach dropped and my own tears started to well up. Typically, I was prepared, armed with a speech, but that day the stress was too much. It had been building for weeks, and the final blow left me speechless. I eventually muttered, "You are so incredibly brave."

"Mom, I know I am, there are just days that I don't know if I want to be brave anymore." I couldn't have agreed with her more.

Stress is not always isolated to a single event. Sometimes, it is a culmination of several. In my running example, I had failed to acknowledge the blanket of stress I woke up under. Stress from moving, worry, and fatigue left me less prepared to tackle daily challenges. Ask yourself what stress you are feeling when you first wake up in the morning. As you begin to see the fluid nature of stress, requiring continual assessment, it will become easier to tackle future challenges.

Add up your scores on frequency, duration, and intensity to understand the severity of your stress:

Frequency (1-6) ___ + Duration (1-6) ___ + Intensity (1-6) ___ =

Severity ____ (Mild 0-6, Moderate 7-12, Critical 13-18)

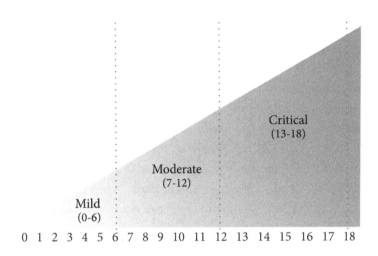

Severity Scale

Reflect: Think of a recent stressful event and consider the dynamic of all three factors associated with your stress (frequency, duration, and intensity). Add your score and note where your total falls on the severity scale. Changing one aspect of this situation can create an entirely different picture.

Experience of Stress

What does not kill you *can* make you stronger, but it can also break you down. Thankfully, the effects of stress are not always negative or damaging. Stress can be a positive experience, such as starting a new graduate program in which you were able to juggle the demands of academic assignments while your spouse was deployed. You are left with a rewarding experience because you were able to rise to the occasion even though it was stressful. The goal of this book is to create more of those experiences! Even the worst days of stress can be tolerable when you rely on coping skills, or find new ones, to get through them.

Seeking Support

When John and I had been married for less than a year, we had our first baby, a beautiful healthy boy we named Luke. This event coincided with my leaving my job and preparing for what would be my first military move—to Germany. Thankfully my mom came and stayed with us ... it was a beautiful and exhausting time. We organized everything, the movers came and went (I distinctly remember hiding in our tiny laundry room to try to keep Luke asleep through all the chaos) and on our final weekend we celebrated a hastily planned baptism so as many family members as possible could be there. When Luke was five weeks old we said goodbye to our entire support network and brought him, along with our sweet old cat, on the harrowing trip to Ramstein, Germany.

It wasn't long before the struggles started to wear on me: jet lag, a tiny hotel room without air conditioning, no comfy rocking chair to nurse him in ... oh, and Luke wouldn't sleep in the portable crib. In the midst of all of this (and likely because of it) my milk supply started to fail me. I would nurse and nurse Luke in the evening and just couldn't give him enough to get him to sleep. We had to resort to supplementing with an evening bottle and it became a nightly need. I just didn't have enough milk.

We had chosen to live off base, and after a week or so in that awful hotel room, we found a house (the first one we toured—we were a bit desperate) and moved in with temporary furniture, in addition to a much-needed washer/dryer and fridge. John got settled into his position at NATO, and I tried to make it through the long, lonely days and nights of taking care of a newborn without household goods or working internet.

One morning as John was heading off to work, I broke down in tears. I told him I couldn't do this. I couldn't spend the day, already exhausted from a sleepless night, alone with the baby in an empty house in a German village where I didn't know a soul. And, to top it all off, I couldn't even make enough milk to feed our baby. It was all too much.

I'm not someone who cries very often, so this breakdown definitely got John's attention. He listened to me, held me for a few moments, and then reassured me he would try to come home for lunch or at least call me to check in, and to hang in there ... it would get better. A few hours later he called me, saying that he had just gotten off the phone with New Parent Support on the base, and that a nurse would be coming over to help me with breastfeeding that afternoon. I was surprised, but so grateful.

That afternoon Joy, a lactation consultant and nurse, listened to my breastfeeding and adjustment struggles, and then she helped me make a plan for slowly reducing the formula I was giving Luke and increasing my milk supply. She continued to visit me weekly for the next couple of months and, once the breastfeeding was going better, she helped me with my overall adjustment. One time she ended our visit by taking Luke and me to the German grocery store across the street, where she introduced me to some of her favorite foods. Another time she mentioned a Fall festival that was happening over the weekend in Bernkastel and encouraged us to check it out (we took her advice and had a wonderful time!). Things got better when our internet was finally connected, we received our household goods, and we made some friends. We even had another baby at the local German hospital eighteen months later.

I've thought many times about what went wrong and what went right about this time in our Air Force life. In retrospect I would have had John make the trip first and get things settled before Luke and I joined him. I probably also would have chosen to live on base rather than in a German neighborhood, even though our neighbors were lovely people. But one thing that definitely went right was the call that John made to New Parent Support and my visits from Nurse Joy. I don't know what we would have done without her. —Molly I., Air Force spouse

As Molly's story shows, the first military move can be a challenging situation in many ways. It was uncomfortable for Molly to move away from family the first time—not to mention being a first-time mom. However, she took a risk and told her spouse how she was feeling. Through this process, she discovered a new resource that helped her cope with not only the struggles of motherhood, but also an overseas move.

The isolation of military life can be overwhelming. Coupled with the stress of trying to find a job, solo-parenting, or adjusting to a new area, it can leave you feeling little hope that things will ever get easier. You may find your old ways of coping aren't working, just like Molly. You may feel stuck, unable to move forward.

The path to getting unstuck from the effects of stress is complex since the effects often blur together. For example, the anticipation of holding a new child brings joy, but perhaps also anxious thoughts about "doing it right." When other factors are present from military life, like giving birth without your spouse or familial support, or being in an isolated location with few resources, it can be more difficult to process. However, just like the frequency, duration, and intensity model used earlier helps to understand the nature of stress, thinking about the effects of stress in terms of positive, neutral, or negative experiences can help you better understand stress's impact in your life.

> **Reflect**: Start to think of the effects of stress in terms of positive, neutral, or negative experience (or combined). Write down:
>
> ~ a positive stressful event, one that left you with a rewarding experience
>
> ~ a neutral, tolerable stressful event, one where you relied upon old coping skills or developed new ones to get through the event
>
> ~ a negative stressful event, one where you felt frozen and were unable to find ways to work through the event
>
> ~ an event that was a combination of positive, neutral, or negative

Milspouse Strength ~ Kendra Lowe

Impact of Stress

Negative or severe stress impacts your well-being on a regular basis even if you don't notice it, so it is important to identify causes and impacts early. Much like a virus, negative stress can take root in your body, attacking many aspects of your well-being. It can break you down little by little or all at once.

If you have a high fever, you might go to the doctor looking for the cause. But what if you have a hard time concentrating or making decisions? What if you cannot sleep through the night or find yourself sleeping all day long? Many military spouses muddle through these signs because we tell ourselves it is still possible, albeit difficult, to get through the day. This mindset leaves us more prone to getting stuck and asking, "How did I end up here?"

If ignored, negative stress can affect you physically, behaviorally, cognitively, socially, and emotionally, and lead to more concerning mental health issues like depression and anxiety.

It is possible to see these signs, or red flags, that stress is beginning to take its toll before you reach a breaking point. Cortisol, commonly known as the stress hormone, releases into your body fifteen minutes after being placed under stress and can remain elevated for several hours. It changes the chemical makeup of your body. Whether it is a single event or a series of events that never seem to end, cortisol is released every time. While it would be great if you could go into the doctor's office and have your cortisol tested as if you had a fever, the more practical and beneficial solution is to learn to self-assess your stress levels and changes to your environment.

Physically, you may notice changes like a lack of energy to get through the day, random headaches, trouble sleeping, or sleeping all day long. Your behavior around coworkers, family or friends may also change, such as arguing with your spouse or children, feeling tempted to drink more than usual, or impulsively buying a new kitchen appliance even though you do not need it. It might be hard to concentrate at work or make decisions because you lose focus. Some days, you may find yourself on the couch crying during a cat shelter commercial when you don't even like cats. If ignored, negative stress can affect you physically, behaviorally, cognitively, socially, and emotionally, and lead to more concerning mental health issues like depression and anxiety.

> **Reflect**: Take note of any common effects of stress you have experienced. Write down how and when you feel these effects most strongly and what coping mechanisms you usually use.

Appearance of Stress

As military spouses, we may weather similar storms of moving, deployments, or un(der)employment, but the impact on each of us is markedly different, therefore stress looks different on each of us.

Avoidance

Take a look at your daily calendar. Is it packed from the moment you wake up until the time you collapse in bed with meetings, tasks, and long to-do lists, leaving very little time to breathe? Avoidance, or actions you take to escape difficult thoughts, feelings, or situations, is commonly seen with military spouses. Over-scheduling yourself creates an environment that leaves you little-to-no free time. Free time you do not want with your thoughts, feelings, or emotions.

Distraction or Destruction?

I am an expert at distracting myself. When I get stressed, I just add more to my plate so I don't have to think about it. I take on a new project at work or I volunteer for another committee at my kids' school—the more the better. I run around so I have less time to sit because when I sit, all I do is think about how much I miss him and my family. I do it out of avoidance, which creates more stress, until eventually everything comes crashing down. I get sick or pure exhaustion takes over, and I find myself hiding in the bathroom, crying on the floor. I just don't know how to stop it because it is the only way I know how. —Amy G., Marine spouse

Avoiding stress does not make it go away, it only pushes it down. If suppressed, stress may enter a dormant state, only to pop back up in a seemingly unexpected way. You could be trying to knock out your grocery list on a busy Sunday morning and find yourself snapping at the person in front of you. The true culprit wasn't really that they took too long, it was the stress of the recent PCS, sitting just below the surface of your mind. Avoidance blocks the opportunity for you to respond to and manage your stress.

Fight or Flight

The fight or flight response is an automatic physiological reaction to an event that is perceived as stressful or frightening. The perception of threat activates the nervous system and triggers an acute stress response that prepares the body to fight or flee. I recall experiencing this during a recent walk in the Colorado mountains, enjoying the blue skies and crisp fresh air with my mother-in-law. As we rounded the corner on the paved driveway, we stood yards away from a slowly approaching black bear. My heart started to race and I could hardly breathe, but my body moved, instantly running back to the cabin before my mind had a chance to kick in and tell me, "The worst thing you can do is run from a bear (or leave your mother-in-law behind)!" The physiological fear triggered a fight or flight response, leaving little to no room for cognitive thought, as I explained later to my family.

As military spouses, we may weather very similar storms of moving, deployments, or un(der)employment, but the impact on each of us is markedly different, therefore stress looks different on each of us.

The physiological responses associated with fight or flight can play a critical role in surviving truly threatening situations. However, many individuals suffering from severe stress may have overactive threat systems that trigger this response and begin to break down the body, even when there is no immediate threat. Over time this seemingly protective measure leaves you vulnerable to future stress.

Freezing

Freezing is often triggered when the fight or flight response is not an option. As opposed to fight or flight, freezing causes your heart rate and breathing to slow down, often leading you to hold your breath. The thoughts you had in your mind just a few minutes ago are nowhere to be found. A job interview presents a great example of this. You enter the building feeling confident, sit down at the conference table, and the interview team starts to ask you very simple questions. The answers you had prepared for weeks suddenly vanish. You are frozen in that moment.

Constant stress can elicit such a response of freezing up or numbing out—disassociating from the present. Under severe stress, you try to "disappear" and block out anything too hard to take in. Freezing can be just as detrimental to your mental health since by nature being stuck or frozen limits your ability to respond to stress.

Anxiety and Depression

Anxiety and depression are often tipping points between functioning and not. I've worked with military families for more than twenty years, and the degree to which depression and anxiety are increasing is concerning. Whether you have dealt with one or both before, or you are unsure if what you are experiencing is anxiety or depression, recognizing symptoms early can help you and others get support.

Depression and anxiety may appear together when you are stressed, making it hard to understand which is which. Depression, or an overwhelming feeling of sadness and despair, is often marked with the loss of interest in things or people around you, particularly during a period of grief. You may start to dread getting together with friends or want to isolate from family. Signs of depression can also be physical, such as struggling to force yourself out of bed in the morning or not showering for an extended period of time. Anxiety, or persistent feelings of worry, can look similar, but the difference is the underlying nervousness, not sadness, that leads you to avoid life events.

Getting Past the Fear

I had wanted and planned for a fourth child and, therefore, was taken completely by surprise when I suffered from severe postpartum after she was born. With no familial support around me, having a baby at thirty-seven turned out to be far more than I imagined. I began to fear everything: she wasn't gaining enough weight, she wasn't sleeping enough. I didn't know when I would ever feel like myself again.

There were days, maybe even an entire week, that I didn't want to leave my home. I forgot to shower on some days and wasn't sleeping. All I did was worry, and yet, I remained unaware of how much I was struggling—that is, until one very memorable Thursday night. A close friend, who was also a military spouse, had heard I was struggling, so she stopped by with another spouse to see me. I admitted to them all the fears I was consumed with daily. The look on their faces told me what I had said was shocking, and yet, it sounded "normal" to me. My friend gently took my hand and said we were all going to the Mental Health Flight right then. They had prearranged care for my two-month-old daughter and would go with me as a walk-in to the appointment. I fought for a good hour, saying I didn't need to go, that it would hurt my husband's career, that I would be labeled as "crazy," and that it could hurt our next assignment if I was "Q coded" with mental health concerns. I pretty much tried any reason I could come up with to get out of going. But they both knew I was severely suffering, and although it was technically possible for one or two of the reasons to come true, my mental well-being was far more important.

They sat with me for four hours that night. We waited to get a walk-in evening appointment, and they never left my side until I was seen by a professional psychologist. The fear of going was eased somewhat when I finally met the psychologist, who led me out of my crisis. It has been a long road with many professionals involved to get me to where I am today.

Anxiety can be debilitating, as I was consumed by thoughts my anxiety controlled. It is different from depression, a difference not many understand.

I started a support group for new moms at our next duty assignment, hoping my experience could help them. Looking back, I wish I had not feared seeking out help, but the reality is that this fear is still alive and well in our military community. We need resources that can reach our spouses when they are unable to reach out themselves. —Nicole F., Air Force spouse

Maintaining an awareness of mental health signs and checking in with the people close to you (including yourself!) allows our military community to heal and get professional help when needed. It is always better to support your mental well-being.

Anxiety vs Depression Symptoms

Anxiety ~ Physical Symptoms

~ feeling fatigued easily

~ difficulty concentrating or recalling

~ muscle tension

~ racing heart

~ grinding teeth

~ sleep difficulties, including problems falling asleep and restless, unsatisfying sleep

Anxiety ~ Emotional Symptoms

~ restlessness, irritability, or feeling on edge

~ difficulty controlling worry or fear

~ dread

~ panic

Depression ~ Physical Symptoms

~ decreased energy, chronic fatigue, or feeling sluggish

~ difficulty concentrating, making decisions, or recalling

~ pain, aches, cramps, or gastrointestinal problems without any clear cause

~ changes in appetite or weight

~ difficulty sleeping, waking early, or oversleeping

Depression ~ Emotional Symptoms

~ loss of interest or no longer finding pleasure in activities or hobbies

~ persistent feelings of sadness, anxiety, or emptiness

~ feeling hopeless or pessimistic

~ anger, irritability, or restlessness

~ feeling guilty or experiencing feelings of worthlessness or helplessness

~ thoughts of death or suicide

~ suicide attempts

Post-Traumatic Stress (PTS)

Stress can also be a response to a traumatic event. Trauma that is felt, experienced, and defined by you. For some this could be the unexpected loss of a loved one, a victim of crime, or surviving a natural disaster. Every time you hear, see, or smell things similar to the event, it triggers an automatic negative response, often leaving you feeling helpless and alone.

As a survivor of post-traumatic stress and years of fighting these feelings, I found peace by shifting the way I defined my experience. Post-traumatic stress is now merely a weakened part of me that requires deliberate and intentional care much like my right knee. After a complete ACL and meniscus tear during a competitive tennis match, I quickly learned that my right knee would never be as it once was prior to injury. I struggled with that fact for many years. What I later learned through acceptance was that I could shift the way I trained. Acknowledging my knee's vulnerability gave me the ability to include targeted weight training to strengthen the muscles supporting the joint. Those muscles currently serve to protect and absorb any future stress.

Post-traumatic stress is an underlying injury that weakens the system, and it flares at seemingly inopportune moments. Those that struggle with this type of injury or stress may require extra care and reassurance that although they may never be as they once were before, they have the ability to strengthen their body, mind, and spirit, all of which serve to protect from future stress.

Each stressful experience is unique and personal. Stress, although complicated at times, can be better understood when you create a lens that allows you to evaluate the source and potential impact. Once you create this lens, it opens up opportunities for more positive stress experiences.

Chapter Reflection

~ Have there been times you believe you were in a negative stress cycle? What effects did this have on you?

~ Note your thoughts about the new stress growth model. What steps can you take today to start incorporating this model?

~ Have you been in a stressful situation that you were unable to see clearly? What were your thoughts afterward?

~ Do you find that you experience more internal or external stress or is it a combination of both? Why do you believe this is the case?

~ Think about your stress in terms of frequency, duration, and intensity. What do you notice about their interaction? What causes the severity to increase for you?

~ Do you notice more positive, neutral, or negative experiences as a result of stress?

~ How does stress typically affect you? Do you try to avoid, enter fight or flight, or freeze?

~ Have you struggled with anxiety or depression? How will you check in with yourself and others to support your mental well-being?

~ How has the word "stress" changed for you? Discuss your thoughts on your new definition of stress with your spouse, trusted friend, or support group.

CHAPTER 2

Self-Assess

Unmask the Aftermath

*Challenges associated with military life are ever-present
and subsequent stress can be significant.*

HOUSEHOLD WORK, PREGNANCY, PARENTING, relationships, a
new mortgage, troubles with in-laws: these are some common life
stressors. There is a good chance you have faced at least a few of them.
As military families, we not only face these common stressors, but
also an amplified version of all of them as a result of the nature of our
military lifestyle. Moving is not an isolated event, but part of a way of
life. It is something you do every two to three years. Household work
takes on a whole new level when your spouse is deployed.

Spinning Plates

*I think that we, as military spouses, are unaware that
we often operate at an elevated level of stress—it's a fact we
sometimes forget. I sometimes visualize stress in my own life like I
am spinning plates; I can keep them going until you add another
plate, and then it all falls apart. Military spouses operate at that
level much of the time. I know I have some of the same concerns
as everyone in the world; I worry about family, money, and
health. But on top of that is this uncertainty about where I am
going to live next, when I will move, if my husband will deploy,
if he is going to be gone TDY, how long he will be gone, and
when he will be back. The addition of these unique stressors is
important for us to acknowledge. I think we tend to tell ourselves,
"I've got this. I've done this before. I can do it again." After
nineteen years of military life and countless moves, every change
is STILL stressful. —Beth A., Air Force spouse*

Beth's story is a reminder that military spouses not only experience personal stress but face additional stressful situations tied to their life in a military family. Many of the challenges military families face, such as deployment or transitioning out of the military, are difficult for others to comprehend because they have never experienced them. Hidden challenges, such as service length, endless cycles of isolation, or contagious stress create unique experiences that bond military spouses. Military families have a shared sense of hope and commitment to family and country that are markedly different from what non-military families experience.

> *Though you wear a brave face of grit, determination, and humility, these unique challenges and experiences are significant.*

Extensive studies have found that military spouses experience significant levels of stress that are sometimes twice as great as the stress levels of spouses married to civilian partners. At any point in time, a substantial portion of military spouses exhibit measurable signs of moderate to clinically significant stress levels. In other words, approximately one in four military spouses wakes up every day under a heavy layer of stress that builds day by day, week by week, and year by year, yet they continue to try to function under this stress.

You might currently be masking the impact of these challenges on your life by telling yourself something like: "I have no right to complain because all military spouses go through it." Though you wear a brave face of grit, determination, and humility, these unique challenges and experiences are significant. They compound the effects of life's common stressors.

"Seen" Challenges of Military Life

In an effort to measure major life events and their potential impact on a person in a year, psychiatrists Thomas Holmes and Richard Rahe developed the social readjustment rating scale. Through extensive research, this scale considers the frequency, duration, and intensity of stress as it relates to these major life events.

However, this commonly used scale leaves gaping holes for military spouses. In the list of common life events used in the scale, most of the "seen" challenges associated with military life are missing and it only gives a snapshot of the past twelve months. Given the nature of military life, it is important to consider a longer duration of time as many of the significant life events noted do not happen just once in a year, but several times over a prolonged period.

Though gauging stress with universal tools such as the one developed by Holmes and Rahe does not work as well for military spouses, applying the model in a similar fashion to the unique challenges of military life does. By using the method discussed in the previous chapter, you can evaluate if you have experienced stress associated with these challenges, how often, and how intensely you felt it, so you can better understand the impact it has on you.

Moving

Moving certainly is not unique to military families. Approximately 15.3 million American households move within a given year and experience the effects of uprooting their lives and adjusting to new communities. The difference for military families is the frequency of this challenge, as most military families move every two to three years, leaving little time to recover from one move before notification of another. By nature, a permanent change of station (PCS) causes the entire family to stop, change direction, and start again (and again and again).

Moving Marathon

Moving is not a short sprint to the next destination, but rather a logistical marathon of emotions. For the months leading up to the move, I find myself in task-oriented mode of purging, organizing, and figuring out logistics. I am physically exhausted. I am also preparing for the goodbyes, either tearing myself away from family and friends or helplessly watching while my children attempt to do the same. I've even found myself pulling away from friends, staying close to home as to avoid another goodbye. I am emotionally exhausted.

Then, the move, where I am truly functioning on superhuman adrenaline. The packers and movers invade my house; I feed them, try to oversee the process, and hope my possessions make it undamaged to my new home. I scrub down the walls and floors and ditch the remains of my refrigerator with neighbors, removing physical evidence that I lived there. The memories and tears present with every turn.

When I finally arrive at my new home, I try to reframe the move as an adventure until it hits. We are bleeding out financially with new curtain rods (the old ones never fit), closing costs, replacing the contents of the refrigerator I just gave away, rugs, a new broom, internet, and bedding in hopes of making my children excited about their new room. I miss friends and the community left behind. The household items arrive, requiring yet another surge of adrenaline to unpack, organize, and play a challenging game of Tetris with my furniture in attempts to make it fit. Mentally I am exhausted.

Eventually, it starts to look and feel like home, and yet there is still something missing. I struggle to find friends, and lack the physical, emotional, and mental energy to try. Internal thoughts of "I hate it here" start to creep in. Then a glimmer of hope. My neighbor invites me to lunch with three of her friends. I laugh for the first time in a while and think "It's not so bad here." Friendships grow into "stand-in" family as they attend my children's birthdays. I start to think "I love this place," which happens to be the exact moment my husband comes home to inform me of our next move. —A., Army spouse

Not all assignments are created equally. There are moves you grow to love, some you merely adjust to, and those you do not like at all. Some moves are overseas and others domestic, some are coupled with the ongoing special medical needs of a child or the birth of a new child. The intensity changes for each move and impacts the stress you feel throughout it.

Reflect: Consider both the positive and negative effects of moving. Challenge yourself to identify positive thoughts, feelings, emotions, or experiences of moving, such as excitement and joy, strong friendships, vibrant community life, or the start of a new job. If moving has been a significant source of stress for you, evaluate the severity. Revisit the first chapter to calculate the effects of the duration, frequency, and intensity on scales of one to six, then add them to get the number representing the severity of your stress. Note any internal stress you might be experiencing associated with moving. Remember: you are in control of your internal stress!

Employment

Moving so often can make it challenging for military spouses to stay on a consistent career path. Because of how often military families move, most spouses must switch jobs every two to three years, which increases the frequency of career stress. Two of the most emphasized challenges among military spouses are staggering unemployment and underemployment, at a rate roughly six times the national average and more than twice the rate in the majority of the country's most impoverished neighborhoods. These rates have held for years despite hundreds of millions of dollars spent by the US Department of Defense (DoD). This ongoing challenge provides little room for professional growth or establishment in a company. In return, companies may shy away from hiring military spouses, leaving military spouses to ask themselves: "Should I even tell them I am a military spouse?"

In addition, more than half of working military spouses say they are overqualified for their current positions. On average, military spouses earn nearly 27 percent less than their nonmilitary peers.

The financial impact can be significant, but even more concerning is the potential impact on self-confidence and self-worth. You update your resume, research a company you're interested in, dig an outfit out of your suitcase, only to be asked: "Can you explain why you haven't worked in the past three years?" Much like a slow leak in a balloon, your confidence begins to deflate as you ask yourself if you are worthy of the job, if you have enough experience, or even if you remember how to do many of the required tasks. You may decide not to interview again, take a salary decrease, or begin to feel helpless.

One of my most memorable interviews happened right after I separated from active duty. I had just moved to Albuquerque, New Mexico, to join my husband after a year separated due to our assignments at two different bases. As I sat down in front of the interview team, one individual inquired: "Why should we select and invest in you for this position knowing you won't stay long?" Although she was right that the remainder of our tour was about a year, I retorted: "I would hope that investing in individuals is the standard for this organization, not negotiable based on job longevity." The room fell silent, and I was not surprised the following week when human resources called to inform me that I was not selected for the position. Meanwhile, Pottery Barn was thrilled to have me on board.

These types of career setbacks can result in a sense of helplessness, or powerlessness, from a perceived failure to succeed. It becomes easier to overlook opportunities and leads to low motivation, low self-confidence, or low self-worth.

Fortunately, unemployment and underemployment does not always cause stress. Many military spouses choose not to work, to stay at home, and support their children or maintain household demands. Others step back from the work environment during lengthy deployments, anticipating the additional demands on their time and energy. Internal thoughts matter for your happiness. "I'm happy I can stay at home for family stability" carries a different weight than "I resent not being able to work while my spouse is deployed." It is important to be content with your decision, whether you choose to work or not.

Deployments and TDYs

Deployments or temporary duties (TDYs) affect each family in different ways, but most military spouses would agree that deployments bring a high severity of stress and require a great deal of perseverance throughout the pre-deployment, deployment, and reintegration phases. TDYs, typically shorter in duration, pose potentially less stress but still require a shift in daily living conditions.

Pancakes for Dinner

I marched down the narrow hallway to give my children their last stern warning to quiet down. Even though it was their standard Friday night sibling slumber party, it was well past bedtime, and I was exhausted. My husband had been TDY for two weeks and although I had endured multiple lengthy deployments, TDYs ended up being challenging as well. The quick shift from having him available one week to absent the next created an environment of constant flux and readjustment.

When he was home, I had become dependent on his support for shuffling kids, errands, housework, and morale support to tackle our crazy schedules.

With him gone, I owned it all, and often struggled to get
through the day without throwing a childish tantrum about
"unbalanced" responsibility. Some rules got bent to alleviate
stress. Pancakes for dinner were worked into meal planning,
mowing the lawn was optional, and bedtime became a loose
phrase implying their mother was officially off the clock. I still
had standards: showers, teeth brushing, and clean clothes were a
must, but I found there are times that I need to just get through
it, and I tell myself that is okay. —Monica L., Navy spouse

TDYs, or what I like to call mini deployments, certainly shift
family dynamics, but deployments are particularly stressful since they
are longer in duration. Deployments are marked with three distinct
phases of pre-deployment, deployment, and reintegration, all with
unique challenges.

For weeks leading up to the deployment, many military spouses
try to manage anticipatory anxiety as they review wills, organize
finances, coach children, and go on outings to favorite restaurants or
hiking trails. Most try to make the best of the last couple of weeks by
creating lists of goals they want to accomplish during the deployment:
paint the bedroom, exercise more, organize the house. Yet the
impending stress is right around the corner, looming over every
minute of the day.

Then comes the deployment, which can seem like an eternity.
By necessity, military spouses become the family decision-maker
responsible for significant issues as well as less consequential family
concerns. With greater responsibility, they have less time to spend
with other family members, namely children. Some may even find
themselves detaching from their children due to the increased
demands on time and daily responsibilities that invariably compete
for attention.

As a spouse muddles through the deployment, knowing it will
not last forever, focus often shifts to the return. Weeks or months
before the end of the deployment, a rush of emotion sets in with
expectations about how the reunion will take place. A new sense
of purpose and energy emerges as the list of goals is pulled out and

reviewed. With nearly superhuman speed, most families try to cram anything and everything all into those last few weeks to complete the impossible and make the reunion perfect. The pending return of a service member can result in fresh stress for the whole family and changes that take place during deployment may result in conflicting feelings about the military member's return.

Welcome Home?

My husband's deployment to Djibouti was extended by two months, so by the time he returned home, I was more than ready. The prepared sign of: "Welcome Home, Happy Birthday!" was crossed out to "Welcome Home, Happy Valentine's Day!" until finally it just became "Welcome Home!" I had painted most of the walls in our home (one of my coping skills); I made curtains and rearranged almost everything, which he later told me drove him crazy. I remember thinking I wanted to make his homecoming perfect but was struggling to know what "perfect" meant. Had I changed too much? Did I change enough? Would the changes affect us?

I drove up north with our two dogs, dropped them off at my in-laws' house, and went to pick up my husband from the airport. I had carefully picked out my outfit, a new pencil skirt and a white blouse. When we returned to his parent's house to get the dogs, our golden retriever lost it when he saw my husband. If I ever doubted the bond of man and dog, it was completely refuted that day, as I had never heard such visceral sounds from an animal. We had dinner at his parents' house before we headed back home. As we entered our home, I was hit by an intense wave of nausea. Resolute that it must have been food poisoning from the takeout, my husband called his parents and discovered no one else was sick, just me. I was sick the entire night and then riddled with guilt. What a shitty welcome home. I recovered quickly the next day and soon realized the stress, anxiety, and anticipation of his return had taken a physical and emotional toll on my body. I was completely unaware that my thoughts could cause such an intense, cathartic release upon his return. —Kate L., Army spouse

The service member returns, marking the start of reintegration. Depending on the length of deployment, this stage may involve significant observable changes. For instance, your spouse may become aware of physical changes in various family members. They may see a toddler walk for the first time, notice a child's missing tooth, or realize how much the child has grown. These changes may be stressful for your service member since they can physically see the changes that took place during deployment that they missed while away. Both service members and military spouses often struggle to adjust to being together again, taking a few days or even months, and going through multiple phases of honeymoon, disillusionment, anger, and acceptance before arriving at a new normal.

Specific tasks associated with successful reintegration include role definitions, expectations, labor division, managing emotions, recreating a new form of intimacy, and creating shared meaning. Even with these proactive actions, military families are seldom prepared for the physical or psychological impact deployment may have upon their family. If left unrecognized and untreated, the issues surrounding homecoming may affect your family for many years. Some of the most important areas to consider are communication, intimacy, and parenting, since these elevate emotions for the whole family (including pets!).

Even when your service member is home, it may feel like you are experiencing deployment. Many service members identify military service as a calling, not a nine-to-five job, and are consumed by their dedication. The constant after-hours phone calls, missed dinners, and late arrivals to your children's school events are regular stress events that place extra pressure on you as a military spouse. These events may slowly wear away at your patience and raise stress levels just like they did during deployment. Your spouse doesn't have to be physically out of the home for you to experience significant stress.

Reflect: Consider both the positive and negative effects of TDYs and deployments. Challenge yourself to identify positive thoughts, feelings, emotions, or experiences from TDYs or deployments, such as contentment, strengthening friendships, or time for personal interests. If deployments or TDYs have been a significant source of stress, evaluate the severity. Revisit the first chapter to calculate the effects of the duration, frequency, and intensity on scales of one to six, then add them to get the number representing the severity of your stress. Note any internal stress you might be experiencing associated with TDYs and deployments. Remember: you are in control of your internal stress!

Retirement and Military Separation

While no one remains a military spouse forever, service-related experiences will forever be part of who you are. This time is but one chapter in your life, and you should be immensely proud of what you have accomplished and overcome. However, the challenges of life do not end once the service member retires. They simply morph into different types of challenges.

A Relatable Narrative

Re-. The prefix is attached to many words in military life. Resilience, reintegration, and retirement are the three words that stick out when I reflect on our military life. Re- is a prefix with a simple meaning: back or again. Resilience, to me, was overused when describing a military spouse but it is an important characteristic in my making it to my spouse's retirement while retaining some sanity. Reintegration was experienced many times over the years due to combat deployments, long TDYs, overseas PCS, and it was different every time. Developing resilience and enduring reintegration were huge factors in preparing me for what I had so long looked forward to … retirement!

Retirement is reintegration. But this time, we were going back to the civilian world, not to normal military life (does normal exist?). This reintegration was unlike any we had experienced before. No matter how ready I was, or thought I was, it was an uneasy feeling for all of us in our own individual way. We gave ourselves our "next assignment" based upon the job my spouse had fortunately lined up working from home (huge adjustment!), so home could be anywhere. We chose a place separate from the military community and family, but it fit our life for many other reasons—cost of living, schools, conveniences, and climate. Exhilarating yet overwhelming. While we saw small appreciations such as veteran parking and veteran/military discounts, other common sightings such as signage for a base or BX/PX were nonexistent. We have now even removed the word commissary from our language and stopped using the twenty-four-hour clock when stating a time for an appointment or meeting.

We definitely met challenges, some expected and some not, along the way to civilian life. Navigating a way to fit into a society that for the most part appreciates your service but doesn't understand your life and sacrifices made for the last twenty-plus years can be daunting. People awkwardly look at you when you start to answer a simple curious question such as, "Where did you move from?" For our family we had to find a relatable narrative, or common ground, about our former life to make friends with neighbors and reconnect with extended family. We forget that most Americans have not moved fifteen times in the last twenty years. People have established friend groups, community involvements, and comforts of which you are now wanting to be included, and your resourceful spouse network is no longer readily available. What was a normal lifestyle to us can now sound boastful just by naming all the places we have lived or traveled. This was especially important and challenging for our kids. At times, they mute their prior life in an effort to fit in but remain proud of it. We have also met challenges with schools and health care providers as they are not always experienced with military families and struggle to translate multiple school records or handle missing medical records that are impossible to obtain.

While I didn't realize it at the time, the experiences and challenges we faced during military life (and how we responded to them, gracefully or not) created opportunities for success in our "final" assignment, retirement. One day, we will feel as though we are truly home. —Meredith H., Air Force spouse

Recently separated or retired military families need to prepare emotionally for the transition to civilian life. You may not have the financial and social support you experienced in the military, and you may find yourself in a cycle similar to the phases of deployment: pre-retirement, retirement, and reintegration into civilian life. As in Meredith's story, the months leading up to retirement or separation involve discussions about jobs, where you could potentially live, finances, logistics, and loss of a familiar way of life.

Once discharged, your service member becomes a veteran. For retirees, your military IDs change. Most former military members who separate before twenty years of service are no longer eligible for a military ID card. This significant transition away from an active military community may cause your service member to experience grief with the perceived loss of their military self as they try to navigate a new identity. It affects you as well. Through all its challenges, military life has become part of your identity, perhaps something you have grown to love. This grief and subsequent stress during the transition from military to civilian life are associated with several mental and physical health problems.

Integration back into civilian communities can elicit a large spectrum of emotions. You may feel excitement and hope when purchasing a home close to family as you envision holidays and birthdays shared with extended family members. This could be mixed with fear and anxiety of leaving military culture behind. There is also a sense of closure as you move on to a new chapter in life, with the freedom of possibility and opportunity. Yet the lingering feeling of loss remains. It's not just a retirement or separation from a job, but a culture and community. Transitioning into civilian life may be even more stressful for military families than reflected by current research.

> **Reflect**: Consider both the positive and negative effects of
> retirement or separation. Challenge yourself to identify
> positive thoughts, feelings, emotions, or experiences
> of retirement or separation (pending or current). If
> retirement or separation has been a significant event
> for you, evaluate the severity. Revisit the first chapter
> to calculate the effects of the duration, frequency, and
> intensity on scales of one to six, then add them to get
> the number representing the severity of your stress.
> Note any internal stress you might be experiencing
> associated with retirement or separation. Remember:
> you are in control of your internal stress!

Fear of Death

Every time your service member leaves for training, TDYs, or deployments you know there is a possibility they might not return. Fortunately, most spouses never have to face the reality of this fear, but it doesn't lessen the ongoing worry and anxiety you face every time their bag is packed and placed next to the front door. The mere sight of it carries intense emotions. On the outside, you may guard yourself for your family's sake, reminding them of your service member's extensive training. But you know there are those who have not returned, and that fear is so real you can hardly breathe.

When your service member is gone, you find yourself tethered to your phone, even balancing it on stacked laundry you're putting away just in case that happens to be the exact moment it rings. You anxiously await phone calls, text messages, or an email letting you know they are still safe. When they do call, nothing else matters except the five-minute conversation that makes up for days of anxiety and apprehension. The connection provides momentary relief from your stress, which is why it can be devastating when you miss that call, leading to feelings of anger, discouragement, or hurt.

Military spouses are immersed in a culture in which friends, squadrons, and units become family. Even when you are not experiencing a current deployment, another close military member's deployment can elicit fear as it can trigger memories of your past deployments or new worry about a pending deployment. There are also times you help carry the emotional weight for fellow military spouses going through a deployment.

> **Reflect**: Consider both the positive and negative effects of fear of death. Finding the positives of this type of stress is exceptionally difficult, but they exist. Challenge yourself to find positive thoughts, feelings, emotions, or experiences, such as cherishing the time you have with your spouse or living a life in which you are grateful each day. If the fear of death (internal) has been a source of stress for you, evaluate the severity. Revisit the first chapter to calculate the effects of the duration, frequency, and intensity on scales of one to six, then add them to get the number representing the severity of your stress. Note any internal stress you might be experiencing associated with your fear of death. Remember: you are in control of your internal stress!

"Hidden" Challenges of Military Life

In addition to commonly discussed and highlighted challenges of military life like moving, deployments, retirement, and fear of death, there are also hidden challenges. The hidden, or unseen, challenges of military life are the daily experiences that wear you down over time and are much harder to notice. Our personal and collective biases about these types of challenges can add blinders, preventing us from seeing significant levels of stress within ourselves and in others.

Length in Service

Adjusting to any new culture creates social and emotional stress as you try to navigate a world of new social, demographic, and personal constructs. The military culture is no exception. Indeed, the military has a distinct culture of its own. As military spouses, we become part of this unique culture the minute we pledge to stand beside, for better or worse, our military service member. Unfortunately, most of us are not prepared for the drastic impact of this new culture we have entered.

New Military Spouses

When you first become a new military spouse, it can feel like moving to another country (and sometimes you do!) or entering a secret club with its own culture, rituals, rules, and unique language that eventually becomes second nature to military families.

Finding My New Identity

I didn't come from a military family, so when I attended my first newcomers' briefing in Okinawa and someone yelled "a-ten-HUT!" when a man with a shiny rank entered the room, I seemed to be the only person in the full auditorium who didn't know what was going on. Of course, I was the last person to stand up, while my heart sank with the realization that I was now in a foreign culture in more ways than one. That's when it hit me just how much I did not know about being a military spouse. I felt very alone. I spent the first few months looking for jobs, trying to make new friends, and desperately trying to figure out how to be a military spouse. I cried, prayed, journaled, and called my family frequently. I didn't know how to interact with a culture full of acronyms and military customs. I didn't know the "rules" of being a military spouse. My husband tried to calm my fears and quiet my insecurities, but it wasn't until I immersed myself in the military spouse culture that things really changed for me.

I spent most of my time overseas establishing my new identity as a military spouse and figuring out the advantages and disadvantages that come with the title. I quickly learned the acronyms TDY and PCS and figured out the differences between the various branches of the military. I learned that no matter how resilient military spouses appear to be, it's still okay for us to feel discouraged when the mission takes priority over family time or when last-minute TDYs disrupt anniversary plans. I discovered the beauty of homecomings after months apart. I learned how

to build strong friendships with spouses quickly. I learned to
stand at attention when the colonel walks into the room at the
promotion ceremony. Most importantly, I learned that I am not
alone, and many military spouses feel exactly like I do.
—Lucy W., Air Force spouse

Entering into an unfamiliar world poses many challenges.
Like Lucy, you might feel like every military spouse you encounter
has it figured out. New military spouses often hesitate to reach
out for senior spouse support because they minimize their stress,
thinking they have no right to complain when others have been
through multiple moves. However, the external stress of moving is
compounded by both entering a new culture and potential internal
stress of loneliness and sadness. It can be just as significant for you as
it is for those who have been part of the military for years.

Seasoned Military Spouses

It may appear like seasoned spouses have it all figured out, but I
assure you their stress associated with military life is still significant.
Seasoned spouses are often praised for being resilient and strong,
yet they too face exceptional challenges over extended periods of
time. This disconnect between what is seen as confident experience
and what lies underneath places extremely high expectations and
increased pressure on senior military spouses who are struggling.
They may not always feel resilient, but this perceived external
expectation prevents them from speaking up.

Stress Is My Constant

It's hard to believe that I have been a military spouse for
twenty-two years. I've seen lots of changes in our military world,
but the one thing that has remained constant is my level of
stress. If anything, my stress has gone up; it's a persistent nagging
in the back of my mind. At the beginning of my marriage, the
stressors were different. I would worry about my marriage being
strong enough to survive the last-minute deployments, missing
that weekly call, or that our kids would struggle with moving

every few years. Now, the struggles are worrying if my spouse will finally reach the point of exhaustion, if my kids will find their own path to happiness, and how I will fit into this current military world.

Being a seasoned spouse makes me feel like I should have all the answers. For example, how to move through the PCS and deployment cycles seamlessly. The only answer I am assured of is to ask for help. After serving as a leadership spouse, making many baby meals and gifts, and providing support and counseling for some amazing families, it's so hard to be the one to ask for help. Being the one with the answers or serving as the go-to person, it's easy to hide behind a facade that says, "We're okay." Asking for help never gets easy. People offer to help, but it's hard to take them up on it. I often realize we find the most joy and fulfillment in helping others. Learning to accept help is more difficult for me than giving it. My circle of peers is smaller now and I've been the helper for so long that asking for help feels odd. I feel like everyone expects me to have the answers and know-how to fix everything. —Jennifer A., Air Force spouse

Military spouses are part of this unique culture from the moment the service member raises their right hand. From that moment on, stress becomes a part of our lives. Many military spouses grow accustomed to stress as part of their military experience. It has been found that military spouses with only a few years of service experience stress levels similar to families with numerous years of service. The underlying causes of stress may change over time, but the cumulative effect of a constant stress environment results in military spouses' overall stress levels remaining constant, regardless of the length of service.

Our personal and collective biases about these types of challenges can add blinders, preventing us from seeing significant levels of stress within ourselves and in others.

Reflect: Consider both the positive and negative effects of being part of the military culture. Challenge yourself to identify the positive thoughts, feelings, emotions or experiences of military culture, such as excitement, curiosity, seeing a new part of the country or world, mentors, or service to your country. If this adjustment to military life has been a significant source of stress for you, determine the severity. Revisit the first chapter to calculate the effects of the duration, frequency, and intensity on scales of one to six, then add them to get the number representing the severity of your stress. Note any internal stress you might be experiencing associated with military culture. Remember: you are in control of your internal stress!

Isolation

You might hear the word isolation and think of a move overseas or families who are separated on unaccompanied tours where military members serve in an area that cannot support family members. Geographic isolation from friends, family members, and familiar communities is highly present within military communities and poses significant external stress. These types of external events are out of a military spouse's control.

Isolation can also involve internal stress, such as military families choosing to live separately due to educational, medical, or social and emotional concerns of family members. These decisions are not taken lightly, as the spouse has to weigh the potential stress associated with being apart against the needs of the family. Social and emotional isolation within military communities is also common.

A military lifestyle feeds the cycle of isolation, as you move, try to connect with new friends and community activities, finally find the perfect fit, and then tear yourself away as you move yet again. There are also times when friends, family, and community surround you, yet you still feel alone.

Isolation's Hold

I get frustrated with myself because I know I am capable and smart, and I hate that I struggle to function. It's maddening. I know there are ways I can feel better and deal with situations better, but I just don't know where to begin. One of my closest friends (another military spouse) invited me to a resiliency weekend over a year ago, and I just couldn't bring myself to go. Reflecting back, I should have gone because it was advertised as a weekend built specifically for military spouses, with motivational speakers, childcare, and even free time. It sounded perfect but for one thing: I had to actually sign up. I had to get out of my house. You see, I had isolated myself for so long that the fear of going and sharing myself with a large group of strangers who would not be there for me in the future was just too much for me to overcome. —Renee S., Marine spouse

It is easy to get trapped in a cycle of isolation that is damaging to your well-being. Research has shown that loneliness and social isolation can be twice as harmful to physical and mental health as obesity. It is important to remember that social and emotional isolation are related to internal stress based on your perception of the world around you, as opposed to geographic isolation, which is likely out of your control. Even within environments that appear to an outsider like they are rich with connections and opportunities, spouses may feel lonely and isolated.

> *Loneliness and social isolation can be twice as harmful to physical and mental health as obesity.*

Reflect: Consider the positive and negative effects if you have been geographically isolated. Challenge yourself to identify the positive thoughts, feelings, emotions, or experiences of being in a remote location, such as contentment, educational opportunities, or preventing another move. If this isolation has been a significant source of stress for you, determine the source and severity. Revisit the first chapter to calculate the effects of the duration, frequency, and intensity on scales of one to six, then add them to get the number representing the severity of your stress. Note any internal stress you might be experiencing associated with isolation. Remember: you are in control of your internal stress!

Exceptional Family Members

Another common but less highlighted stress associated with military life is caring for special medical or educational needs of family members. The Exceptional Family Member Program (EFMP) was established in the early 1980s to help military families who have members with such needs. This program supports children, spouses, or dependent adults of active duty personnel. Once enrolled in EFMP, families can receive information on community services, related education, referrals to other professional providers, local school and early intervention services, case management, and specialized plans. Even with these robust programs, many families in need do not enlist in available support due to a fear that self-identifying could impact assignments or promotion rates.

Special Child, Special Needs

My son has a neurological disorder that directly impacts his life and well-being as well as our military family. At times, it is extremely frustrating to get him standard specialty care when it is so readily available in the States. As much as we love the military and love being overseas, I look forward to the day we can make our child's needs a priority without the limitations of an overseas

base. We look forward to choosing a home that has access to
groups and peer supports with kids more like him.
—Ashley M., Air Force spouse

Whether military families choose to enroll or hesitate, the stress remains. Moving takes on a different level of stress when you have to coordinate specialists for your children, collect records from multiple locations, retell medical or educational history yet again, and possibly undergo more testing if the new specialist requires it. As Ashley noted, it can feel like a conflict between staying in the military and finding better care. Given these ongoing concerns, it is not surprising that spouses in families with special educational and medical needs exhibit higher levels of stress.

Reflect: Consider both the positive and negative effects of caring for a family member with special needs while moving with the military. Challenge yourself to identify positive thoughts, feelings, emotions or experiences. If caring for a family member with special needs has been a significant source of stress for you, determine the source and severity. Revisit the first chapter to calculate the effects of the duration, frequency, and intensity on scales of one to six, then add them to get the number representing the severity of your stress. Note any internal stress you might be experiencing associated with caring for a family member with special needs. Remember: you are in control of your internal stress!

Stress Contagion

Unfortunately, stress can be quite contagious. The stress you feel associated with military life is impacted by those around you and the way they react to stress. Stressful experiences from the peripheral people and communities in your life can still affect your stress levels, even if the experiences themselves do not involve you. Current research with mothers and infants reflects that infants can "catch" their mother's physiological stress through simple interactions, without exposure to the stress itself. The same holds true for your children, spouse, and community: their stress can spread to you, so it is important to maintain a home and school environment where you can process your own stress separate from everything at once.

Military Children

Military children on average move every two to three years and change schools at twice the rate of civilian children, so they also experience significant social and emotional stress. They are particularly vulnerable to such stress since they are early in their emotional and physical development. It can be a struggle to talk to kids about adult feelings and emotions, but the conversations are important. Military kids are forced to deal with these feelings frequently at an extremely young age.

I have experienced this over and over again with my own children, and one time in particular stands out to me. I paused at the doorway and heard my older daughter lead prayers for her sister and brother. "Our Father, Who Art in Heaven …" they chimed together. My heart swelled in a brief moment when I felt like I wasn't completely failing as a parent. Not wanting to let that moment go, I remained outside the doorway to listen to their post prayer conversation, which was typically entertaining.

"Gabe, why aren't you wearing your pajama shirt tonight?" my daughter questioned.

"Men don't wear pajama shirts, so I'm not wearing them anymore. Plus, it's hot here in Texas. Today my knee armpits were even sweating!" my seven-year-old son replied.

"What is a knee armpit?"

"You know, that place behind your knee. It sweats like crazy here!"

The girls laughed and told him they were going to tell their Dad about the "knee armpit" when he got home.

"We should say a prayer for Dad too," my second daughter suggested.

My oldest, taking charge, led her prayer. "Dear God, we know our Dad has to be away to help fight for our country, but please keep him safe. Watch over him while he jumps out of helicopters and trains to get the bad guys. We know he is doing important things, but we need him to come back safe to us. We need him to wrestle Gabe, so he doesn't attack us. We need him to make waffles in the morning because Mom's are terrible with the applesauce. We need him to hug us tight at night and tell us he loves us. God, we just need him. Amen."

"How long will he be gone?" my son asked.

"As long as he needs to be," my second daughter replied.

"But, what about us?" he probed.

"He loves us very much, but we let them have Dad so other people are safe. That's just what we do."

Not letting any answer suffice his curiosity, he asked one final question, "What if he gets hurt and doesn't come home?"

"Then we have to give him to God."

***

Military children are asked to sacrifice a lot: critical bonding time while a parent is deployed (or unavailable due to long work hours or emotional distancing), childhood friends when they move, and their homes as they start over in an unfamiliar place. Throughout the journey, they are asked to be emotionally stable and adjusted. We hope they spontaneously figure out how to cope with the unique challenges of being a military child. When they struggle, we find ourselves scrambling for ways to help them and looking for where to start. School counselor? Psychologist? Military and Family Life Counselor (MFLC)? Clergyperson? Emergency Room? Primary care physician? Relative? A book? Which book? When you finally pick a direction, doubt creeps in. Will they be mad? Will they go to an appointment? Will this affect the service member's job or assignment? Should I avoid documenting this? What if this gets worse?

The stress your child feels unquestionably affects you too.

Service Member

Service members across all jobs, ranks, and titles, are also confronted with stress that can build week by week, day by day, or even moment to moment. They juggle the demands of not just a job, but a calling that can take them away at a moment's notice for the mission, unit, or people they support. They are repeatedly asked to prioritize the job over family, creating an environment riddled with lack of control and choice. Not least of the demands, there are vastly documented cases of Post-Traumatic Stress Disorder (PTSD), anxiety, depression, and suicidal ideation that plague both current service members and veterans.

Much like the way you experience stress, it's tough for them to flip the "military switch" off when they come home. You may see fatigue in their eyes, frustration in their comments, or a lack of interaction or communication. It is painful to want to relieve their stress and help carry it while being unable to.

Do Not Expect a Life Free From Suffering

Unfortunately, the military has not adequately equipped its members with the cognitive or behavioral tools to navigate the transitions between two fronts: the home front and war front. It is also unfortunate that the family typically bears the brunt of this oversight. The following are lessons I've learned … the hard way.

If your spouse does not, or will not, share their war experiences with you, do not take it personally. Sometimes they are lost in their head, reliving particularly nasty experiences, and the last thing they want to do is give it more power by giving voice to it (right or wrong). Additionally, they may not share because they simply do not want to lay the burden of those experiences on you; it is theirs to carry, not yours. Silence can be a gift.

Your spouse may not know how to "turn off" and is struggling with the transition between warrior and spouse. Give them space, and recognize they are relearning to some extent what it means to be a parent or partner. The attributes that make a great warrior typically make a terrible spouse, and the instincts that have been honed over months of combat are not so easily set aside. Coax them back into the family. They want to be there but carry baggage that was not there before. Like you, they are trying to figure out how to fit it all into a new lifestyle.

Accept that change is inevitable. The nature of your relationship will (and should) change as each of you change, based on your experiences. It is important to remember that the military member may have experienced significant events during their service that will have an impact on them. Do not hold overly tightly to the past, but embrace the present and accept your relationship as it is now. Not all trauma is detrimental or permanent. It just means you have experienced part of life and now have a choice. You either cower down and let those experiences bury you or climb atop them and gain strength and perspective. The same holds true for the military family as you face tribulations and hardships together. The secret is this: do not expect a life free of suffering, but rather choose to overcome the suffering—together. —CMSgt Nathan C., Air Force

Community

When stress is prolonged or chronic, intense, and uncertain in duration, it has increased severity. Natural disasters, environmental contamination, tragic accidents, acts of violence, or pandemics are all examples of events that lead to this kind of stress.

In these situations, stress spreads to community members as they bear witness to environmental or human degradation. For the most part, those within close proximity feel stress more acutely, but this is not always the case for military life. Military families are fortunate to forge friendships, relationships, and community ties all over the world. When you hear news of a category four hurricane impacting Florida, you automatically pick up the phone to call or text the military families you know are stationed there and anxiously await their reply that they are safe, regardless of where you are currently stationed. The community stress military families feel is not always localized to where they reside; it is often spread out throughout their connections around the world. Remaining deeply connected to these people and places is a good thing, but it often means taking on their stress as your own too.

Then there is community stress unique to the military, such as increased deployments, military accidents, withdrawal from lengthy combat missions, or deaths. Hearing news of a tragic helicopter crash overseas certainly draws the attention of civilians, but in a far less significant way compared to military families. Military families are connected to those affected through mutual friends, shared duty stations, or specialized units. It evokes memories of those gone too soon and elicits fears about loved ones, increasing your stress.

I recall one such experience while living in Japan. As green feet started flashing across social media, I knew immediately what that meant … lives lost in our special operations community. Even though I found out these brave individuals were not assigned to our unit, I still felt the impact. Many of the military members in my husband's unit had been stationed with them. Moments later, my husband called: "Kendra, we are gathering the squadron tomorrow afternoon for a small memorial for those lost in the helicopter crash, can you please post on the spouses page to invite them?" With a new job to do, I moved forward and set my fears aside.

Stressful experiences from the peripheral people and communities in your life can still affect your stress levels, even if the experiences themselves do not involve you.

At the memorial, several service members stood up to recount stories of times shared with those lost. Finally, the senior enlisted manager stood to give the final toast. He paused as his voice started to shake. No longer able to go on, a teammate stood up and gently placed his hand on his shoulder. He looked at the crowd and said the powerful words unique to this community: "these things we do … so others may live." A spouse sitting close to me reached out and squeezed my hand. Without words, we both knew the significance of their job and the potential costs that went with it.

Reflect: Consider both the positive and negative effects of stress contagion. Challenge yourself to identify positive thoughts, feelings, emotions or experiences of stressful situations with your children, spouse, or community, such as bonding with your child or spouse through experiences, community connection, opportunities to help, or service to a greater cause. If contagious stress has been significant for you, determine the source and severity. Revisit the first chapter to calculate the effects of the duration, frequency, and intensity on scales of one to six, then add them to get the number representing the severity of your stress. Note any internal stress you might be experiencing associated with the stressful experiences of others. Remember: you are in control of your internal stress!

This chapter highlights commonly seen and hidden challenges associated with military life, but it should not be considered comprehensive. There will be scenarios specific to your life and yours alone. I encourage you to think deeply about where the stress in your life comes from and how it manifests. The goal is to appreciate both positive and negative effects of challenges associated with military life, self-assess stress that affects you, and determine potential severity so you can start on the path to managing stress better. By identifying your stress, you can gain clarity and find the methods of managing it that are best for you and your family.

Chapter Reflection

~ Research reflects that one in four military spouses could be experiencing clinical levels of stress. Were you surprised by this number? Why or why not?

~ Review the positive aspects you noted associated with challenges in military life. Describe how these are "positive stress experiences."

~ Look back on the various stressors you identified in your life associated with the military. Reflect on how it makes you feel to see them all on the page. Is it overwhelming or satisfying? Do some categories of stress show up more often than others? Write down the scores you calculated and add them together.

~ In general, the higher the number you calculated for severity of stress, the more likely you are to have a stress-induced health related event. If you identified a lot of high severity stressors in your life, what steps will you take this week or month to help promote your well-being and bring you more joy?

~ Of the examples you noted in this chapter, is most of your stress external or internal? Why might this be the case?

~ Of the stress you noted in this chapter, is most of it "seen" or "unseen" stress associated with military life? Take particular care to reflect on the "unseen" stress (length in service, isolation, exceptional family members, and stress contagion). Discuss your reaction to these stressors with your spouse, a trusted friend, or a support group.

~ How has your understanding of the challenges associated with military life changed since you started this book? Take a moment to appreciate your growth and progress.

CHAPTER 3

Respond

Think About Thinking

*The mind is an extremely powerful tool that
you can train to work for you or against you.*

THE FIRST DAY OF GRADUATE WORK, my professor announced to
the class that we were going to spend the next three hours "thinking
about our own thinking." An audible groan followed as most of the
class was not excited about the idea of taking a peek inside their own
head. Much to our professor's pleasure, we later discovered that great
power lies within the ability to control your mind.

Understanding and assessing stress, although important steps, are
not the greatest predictor of whether you thrive as a military spouse.
Despite the often unpredictable and uncontrollable circumstances
of military life, it is important to acknowledge you are in control of
how you respond to stress both emotionally and behaviorally. This
control can be achieved through building a rational view of your
environment and evaluating your stress response based on your
thoughts, emotions, and behaviors. Controlling your response to
stress promotes positive stress experiences and leaves you better
prepared for any life challenge.

Salty or Sweet?

*I had a military spouse reach out to me looking for advice
"from someone who has done this longer." She was struggling with
the sacrifices she and her family continue to make while serving
in the military. She was feeling "salty" (her word choice) toward
the military and wondering if the military really cared about her
and her family. In her email she asked, "What keeps you going?*

What makes it okay for you to continually make the sacrifices for your spouse's career?"

Sound familiar? I think we can all relate, questioning whether the sacrifice is worth it and whether anyone really does care. Ultimately, each family needs to decide what is best for them, but my advice to her was to reframe her thinking. Life as a military spouse is not easy, and our families do sacrifice a lot. It is okay and completely normal to feel "salty" at times toward the military and this lifestyle, but the key to being able to keep going is to not allow yourself to stay there. We should absolutely acknowledge the "suck" but then shift our focus on more positive thoughts.

Learning to reframe our thinking can completely change our outlook and prevent self-destructive thoughts that lead to bitterness and anger. Thinking on those things you know to be true and focusing on how you can make a difference in your life, your family's life, and those around you, can make all the difference in how you view this military life. And for that spouse who was seeking advice: she realized that although she did not choose this life, she did have a choice about whether she embraced it, making it a "sweet" experience. —Leslie J., Air Force spouse

Understanding responses to stress can help you cope with the stress you feel today and prepare for the stress you will feel tomorrow—an inevitable part of military life. The goal is to build a toolkit that allows you to sidestep stressful situations quickly and avoid feeling frozen, depressed, or anxious. These self-help tools have proven long-term results when performed consistently and intentionally.

Thoughts → Emotions → Behaviors

"Why did you do that?"

"Because I felt like it!"

Sometimes we really do feel like it and our actions become the product of our emotions. This seems like a simple concept, but the specific link between feelings and actions is not always clear.

Suppose you are late picking your child up from school. As you drive down the street, you might be thinking: "I'm going to be late, and they are going to be upset." This naturally produces anxious thoughts, causing you to put your foot down on the pedal and drive a little bit faster, not noticing the cop car behind you. The interaction between the thought of being late and its emotional response results in the action of speeding. Actions are not isolated behaviors, but rather the product of your thoughts and feelings.

You create your emotions based on how they are experienced. It is possible to change how you feel and behave by making specific changes to your thinking. For example, when you feel an emotion, you first perceive the situation. Perception is the interpretation of signals sent to your brain by your sense of touch, smell, taste, sight, or hearing. Next, you think and believe something about those perceptions. Finally, you have a gut feeling related to your thoughts. In the example of being late to pick up your child, noticing the time influences your thoughts, which then influences your emotions, and finally results in a negative behavior.

> *It is possible to change how you feel and behave by making specific changes to your thinking.*

Perception: You see what time it is and you perceive you are going to be late picking up your daughter from school.

Thoughts: You think your daughter is going to be upset with you.

Emotions: Your thoughts make you feel anxious.

Behavior: You drive faster.

Understanding stress is a thinking exercise, so it helps to examine the relationship between thoughts and actions another way. Most people do what they think is right for them at the time. You might regret driving faster to pick up your child and feel frustrated about the subsequent speeding ticket, but while you were in the moment—accompanied by strong emotions—it seemed like the right thing to do. These strong emotions are deceptive, clouding your ability to think and disrupting core decision-making skills. Maintaining an awareness of your emotions is so important because it clears your vision and creates space for greater acceptance of yourself and others.

Choose to Shift Focus

Military spouses have very little control over the events that affect our lives. Unlike civilians, moving isn't a matter of if but when. Grasping for control is difficult within a culture where change is constant. However hard it may be, it is possible. Shifting your focus from the event (pending move) to your response is the point where you can take back some of that control. You do have a choice in how you perceive, feel, and act when faced with stressful events. Emotions and behaviors are the result of your mind's interpretation of events, so thinking a move will be a great opportunity or the worst situation possible is determined by you and within your control.

Choosing Joy

For the first twenty-eight years of my life, I had it pretty darn amazing. I grew up in a military home with two loving parents and a fantastic sister. I earned a scholarship to attend the out-of-state school of my dreams, entered into the military myself, and eventually met and married Jeremy Fresques, the man of my dreams. A little over a year after getting married, Jeremy was killed in Iraq. My whole life was suddenly and unexpectedly flipped on its head. As painful as this experience was, I knew I didn't want to become the poor, depressing widow no one wanted to be around. … I chose to meet other widows who had been through it and also maintained a positive attitude. I leaned on my faith, attended conferences, joined grief groups, and did things (hello, skydiving!) my husband had wanted me to do. I used my situation to brief incoming wing and group commanders about notification procedures so hopefully other future widows and widowers would have the most dignified experience they could. Knowing I could help someone else made my situation have some purpose and, in effect, gave me healing. I didn't want the fact that I was a widow to define me. It is not who I am, but it is something that happened to me.

After all these years and experiences, I am still surprised at how a good attitude can make a real difference. For example, when we arrived to Okinawa and our household goods were delivered, we found out the moving company lost almost 2,000 pounds of our belongings. Unfortunately, the majority of our lost items were irreplaceable, sentimental items, including the flags from Jeremy's coffins, his beret and boots, and the last possessions of his I owned. The moving company lost around 400 Christmas ornaments that were the love gifts my parents gave every year, representing all of our interests and travels. It was extremely difficult to focus on all of the missing items as we filed our claim. Instead of letting it drag me down, I chose to focus on the perspective. In the grand scheme of things, the missing items are just things. God taught me some good lessons about being attached to possessions.

It might be the life experiences I have gone through or watching others, but I have definitely found life to be much more enjoyable when you choose joy. Life will always give you plenty of opportunities to show you what you are made of. Difficult times are inevitable, but there is always a choice for how you respond.
—Lindsey R., Air Force spouse

Lindsey's response to this tragic event is remarkable, and it reflects that there is always a choice in how we respond to events outside of our control. Angry thoughts will make angry feelings, depressed thoughts will make depressed feelings, and happy thoughts will make happy feelings. Much like traveling through military life, these thought paths can be unpredictable with quick turns, and that is okay. Growth stems from the recognition of your initial thoughts, balancing your response, and ultimately shaping your actions based on controlled thought.

Initial Response

Much of the news we receive as military spouses comes unexpectedly, with little time to plan or prepare—leading us to believe the only constant we have is change. As a result, our initial thoughts about change are usually somewhere close to frustration, fear, or possibly even anger. Initially, it is hard to adjust to a lifestyle full of change. For me, this was particularly true during my husband's deployment to Yemen.

I wasn't allowed to tell anyone my husband was there, at the embassy in Yemen. The only person who knew was my brother-in-law, Matt, a USAF HH-60 pilot at the time. As far as everyone knew, my husband was deployed again to an unknown location. They accepted this as normal and rarely asked questions, knowing those kinds of questions only created more anxiety for me.

Having decided to visit my family that summer, I woke up early and shuffled down my mom's spiral wooden staircase to get a cup of coffee. Our baby was only two and a half months old and was still waking up several times a night, so I was looking forward to a warm cup of caffeine. My mom, a lifelong early riser, was already in the kitchen, beautifully dressed with makeup on and ready to conquer the day. I, on the other hand, looked like I had just stepped out of a bar fight with my shirt inside out, unbrushed hair, and dark circles under my eyes. I nodded a quick hello that cautioned it was too early for conversation. I slowly poured a cup of coffee and walked into the adjacent living room, where Fox News was broadcasting.

"We don't want another Benghazi, so twenty-one embassies have been ordered to evacuate." I bit my lower lip. Given the nature of my husband's job, I knew he would have to stay; he would be the last out, so others might live. I listened to the rest of the report and tried not to react in front of my mom for three reasons: (1) I was instructed not to share his location, (2) confiding in her would not absolve my worry but only add to her own, and (3) it would only confirm my mother's desire for us to stay longer. I could only handle so much togetherness.

Not wanting to cancel our plans for the day, we arrived at the American Girl doll store about midafternoon. While my older girls stood in the store deliberating on which set of matching pink pajamas they wanted, my phone rang. I stepped out of the store briefly to take the call.

"Kendra, it's Matt. I know he's there, and he is safe right now. He won't be able to contact you because he has gone underground. I want you to know we will get him out. He won't be left behind."

My whole body shook; I could barely breathe. The recurrent worst-case scenario image popped into my head: a blue, official car waiting outside my house. Before Matt's call, I could imagine it sitting there, knowing what the military officials were waiting to tell me. I imagined I would drive by them, pull into my garage, unload the kids, and hide. They would knock, and I would brace myself for a blow I knew I would never recover from.

Our initial responses or thoughts work similarly to how cortisol is released immediately into our body once presented with a stressful situation. When I received that phone call from Yemen, the anxious thoughts of my husband flooded in before I had a chance to process them, let alone control them. Your initial thoughts about a situation (whether positive, neutral, or negative) are natural, part of experiencing stress. Accepting that you cannot control these initial thoughts gives you the grace to feel the way you need to feel at that moment. Do not deny these thoughts.

> **Reflect**: Think of a past stressful experience. What initial thoughts did you have during this time? Write them down and evaluate what actions you took based on those thoughts.

Three Thought Paths

Your initial thoughts are real, and they are not always pleasant, but they do not have to last forever. After the initial wave, you have the opportunity to pause and consider the situation through a different lens. You can reframe the initial unpleasant thoughts to more positive ones. Before you work on reframing, though, it is important to have a deeper understanding of the three thought paths and how they drive feelings, emotions, and behaviors.

Using an example of a deployment that has been moved up two weeks, below are the positive, neutral, and negative thought paths that could occur:

Positive thoughts about a pending deployment create positive feelings and let you take charge of actions. For example, you might think, "it's two weeks earlier, but not the end of the world" or "this is difficult for us, but I have done this before and I can do this again." Positive thoughts are different from "toxic positivity," or pretending to act happy or cheerful when you are not. Comments such as "everything is great!" denote a superficial mask that covers up genuine thought and can lead to denial, minimization, or invalidation of your real situation. Positive thoughts reflect your current experience, validate your feelings, and connect to a positive outlook.

Positive thoughts can lead to positive actions. Upon learning about the bumped-up deployment, you could make the best of the time you have together and choose fun activities with your spouse before the deployment. You could also make a list of projects you wish to accomplish during the deployment. Maybe it is time to tackle the beige dining room you disliked from the moment you set foot in the house. You could even set up a countdown calendar until your spouse returns and plan monthly goals and adventures to keep you motivated.

Neutral thoughts about an earlier deployment lead to calmer feelings and planned-out actions. Neutral thoughts are not the same as apathy, or lack of emotions and caring, but rather are a set of balanced thoughts that appreciate the positive and negative observations of a situation. Comments such as "this wasn't what I expected, but I will make the best of it" or "I am disappointed I don't have more time with my spouse, but I know this was out of our control" create balanced thoughts that lead to healthy habits.

It is okay to acknowledge feelings of frustration, sadness, or disappointment. The key is to focus on the proactive behaviors you will take in response to those natural feelings.

Neutral thoughts balance disappointment with rational thought. It is okay to acknowledge feelings of frustration, sadness, or disappointment. The key is to focus on the proactive behaviors you will take in response to those natural feelings. Telling yourself "I will make the best of it" honors the challenges you are facing and encourages you to reach out to friends and family for support. Maybe you have seen a counselor in the past and decide to make an appointment or finally reach out to the military family life counselor you met at the squadron and never followed up with. You might even brush up on coping skills that have helped in the past, such as exercise, journaling, or meditation.

Negative thoughts about a pending deployment can lead to angry or depressed feelings and often irrational and isolating actions. Thinking "I needed those two weeks; this is the worst thing that could happen" is an example of what some people call "awfulizing" the situation. Awfulizing, or imagining the situation to be as bad as it could be, leads to resentment toward others.

Thinking the bumped-up deployment is the worst thing that could happen to you affects not only your emotions, but also how you behave toward the people around you. If your mindset about the deployment remains filled with pessimism, you will likely end up isolating from family and friends, worsening your negative thoughts and feelings. Many spouses avoid being around others for fear of what they will say, or they choose to participate in unhealthy activities they think will help them feel better. Drinking more than usual to numb the pain, spending money you do not have, or eating foods you normally avoid are all common negative behaviors stemming from these awfulizing thoughts. It is natural to think they will make you feel better, and sometimes maybe they do, just for a moment, but they also leave you far more prone to long-term problems. Awfulizing leads to a whole lot of "I shouldn't have done that."

It is important to distinguish between negative thoughts and negative or unhealthy behaviors. Negative thoughts are not themselves a problem, and truthfully they are quite common. The problem arises when you begin to believe these thoughts are your reality and are true. Recognizing negative thoughts when they happen will allow you to take proactive measures to shift them toward more neutral or positive outcomes.

Are your thoughts positive, negative, or neutrally balanced? The following keywords and phrases, or red flags, can be signs that negative thoughts are present.
- It—"it" doesn't upset you. You control the way you feel.
- What if—If it happens, you will do the best you can.
- Awfulizing—It is not life or death, only inconvenient.
- Absolutes—Always and never rarely reflect reality.

- I should—Try using "will." If you think it is best, go for it and be confident.
- I have to—You don't have to. You choose to. You are powerful when you make choices.
- Inferior—Making mistakes does not mean you are inferior. It shows you are human. Every time you make a mistake, you learn and grow.
- Hard—Changing is not impossible, but it does require effort. Old habits are tough to break.
- Try—Trying doesn't help. Doing is your superpower. Give it your best.
- Can't—You can if you want to. Do what is necessary. Do what brings you joy.
- Yes, but—You are likely justifying keeping your old habits or avoiding the inevitable. Be confident in your "yes."
- I have to, but I can't—If you can't, then you probably don't have to.

It might seem silly to reframe a few phrases or thoughts, but it really does make a difference. Reframing your mindset about negative thoughts can be tough, much like starting a new exercise routine. As the alarm goes off on a groggy Monday morning, your thoughts kick in before your body moves to get out of bed:

"I didn't sleep that well last night, I should just stay in bed."

"Ugh, it's raining outside, I do not want to run in the rain."

Like exercising, it is often much easier to wake up and tell yourself you do not have enough time or energy to get it in today. You tell yourself, "Surely one missed day will not hurt." The reality is, you probably did get enough sleep and you are already awake. You can go exercise. Yes, it is raining, but you can run in the rain. Something is always better than nothing. Your mind is an extremely powerful tool you can train to work for you or against you.

Obstacles

Understanding the three thought patterns provides a foundation for reframing your thoughts, however much like stress itself, it can be complex. The source and severity of stress can impose significant obstacles when trying to shape your thoughts. It is probably easier to improve thoughts about a pending short move than it is thoughts about a lengthy overseas deployment. When stressors combine together and increase severity, you may need help from others to reframe your thoughts.

Asking for help is not always easy, but it is normal and extremely important. I had a vivid experience of asking for help ten days after my second daughter was born. That day, a US Ch-47D military helicopter with the call sign Extortion 17 was shot down, killing all thirty-eight people on board. It was the greatest single-incident loss of American lives in Operation Enduring Freedom—Afghanistan. Three of those Special Operations airmen were assigned to my husband's unit. It shook our community to its core, a true emotional blunt-force trauma.

On our drive home after the emotional ceremony, my husband turned to me and informed me that he had to deploy to Afghanistan, to the same location, to support the same mission. I was devastated, but I could manage nothing more than "okay" as I tried to accept this unexpected deployment. As we stood in our bedroom and held our farewell embrace, I remember thinking, for the first time ever, "He might not come home." I could barely breathe. We both knew this goodbye was different from the rest. I told him with very little confidence that I would survive, that things would be fine. His response to me was: "I don't want you to just survive this; I want you to CRUSH this." Days later, he deployed.

A week into the deployment, I took our dog Lexy to the vet for her scheduled ACL reconstruction, spurred by a freak accident at a local dog park (who knew dog parks could be dangerous?). We had originally scheduled her surgery before we knew of my husband's deployment, and I considered rescheduling it but knew it could not wait the five months until he returned.

After a successful surgery, we brought our dog home and made her comfortable in our master bathroom with her awkward white cone. I tucked in my toddler, nursed my new baby, and climbed into bed. Around midnight, I woke up to the sounds of crying. Assuming it was my infant girl, I went to pick her up and soon realized it was not the sounds of an infant at all, but rather a whimpering dog. I trudged down the narrow hall and peered over the wooden baby gate into the master bathroom. There was blood everywhere. I blinked my eyes several times, hoping I was still in a dreamlike state, yet the blood remained. Our dog had somehow managed to remove the staples from her left leg, and the gaping wound was bleeding everywhere. I climbed over the gate, found a bandage in our linen closet, and wrapped her leg. I surveyed the bathroom and started cleaning. Then I heard it, this time definitely infant cries, and knew it was time to feed my baby. I climbed over the baby gate again, changed out of my bloodstained pajamas, and fed her. At that point, the dog whimpered louder. Then I heard new crying sounds. All the noise had woken up my oldest, so she was in the master bedroom, crying with outstretched arms, wanting to be held. I clearly remember thinking I was positively NOT crushing this deployment; I was barely surviving the relentless setbacks.

Early the next morning, I loaded the girls into the car to head to the veterinary clinic. When we arrived, I unbuckled my three-week-old daughter, walked into the building, and, like any good mother, handed her to the receptionist. My oldest followed closely behind me, and I told her to sit on the black leather couch. I went back outside to the car and gathered Lexy into my arms and carried her into the reception area while we waited to see the veterinarian. When we were called back into the examination room, the doctor took one look at my crew and his face affirmed what I thought: we were a train wreck. He assessed Lexy's leg and gently told me that he needed to keep her at the clinic to care for her. I reluctantly let go of her red leash and carried the girls back to the car. I cried all the way home. I felt like a failure. I could not even meet our dog's basic needs.

The clinic called daily to provide reports on how Lexy was improving, and yet, I kept telling myself how much I had failed her. After ten days, she was ready to be released, and we were all eager to pick her up. I collected her favorite stuffed duck and we drove to the clinic. When the doctor emerged from the back with Lexy, he asked if it was okay to remove her plastic cone, as they had formed a bond. I agreed and graciously thanked him for his tender care of Lexy. I then looked around and asked where to settle the bill. My husband and I had discussed the ten-day stay, knowing it would be expensive but also the right choice for our family. The doctor paused, looked at me, and said, "Your husband is deployed, right?"

"Yes," I replied.

"This one is on us. It is the least we can do for a family that is serving our nation."

Tears welled up in my eyes and I could not speak for a few moments. I finally uttered, "Thank you," and hugged him. I left the clinic for the second time in two weeks, barely able to navigate the car through my tears, this time tears of joy.

If I could have learned how to ask for help when I was faced with insurmountable challenges, I would not have endured nearly as much stress. I hope you learn early on in your military spouse journey what took me far too long to figure out.

Some events that happen to you, or around you, are out of your control. You cannot change the fact that the military is moving you again, less than a year out from your previous move. I did not choose to have Lexy need medical care, it just happened. These types of events generate external stress that cannot always be managed by simply adopting a more positive outlook. Sometimes, they require support and resources from your community to help you take the first steps toward a better tomorrow.

> *Internal stress, caused by your own thoughts, feelings, and expectations, is usually within your direct control and provides a prime opportunity to shape thoughts into positive or neutral paths.*

On the other hand, internal stress, caused by your own thoughts, feelings, and expectations, is usually within your direct control and provides a prime opportunity to shape thoughts into positive or neutral paths. The pending move could elicit initial thoughts of apprehension or fear, but you can pause, challenge those thoughts, and focus on the positives of being exposed to a part of the country (or world) you have never seen.

As with earlier techniques, the severity of your stress can be measured by frequency (how often), duration (how long), and intensity (how much you feel it). The first time your air conditioner breaks while your spouse is deployed (low frequency, low duration), it creates a low level of stress. You could have initial thoughts of frustration, but once the air conditioner is fixed, these thoughts quickly dissolve. In fact, they might be gone so quickly you do not even need to shape them into positive thoughts. However, when the air conditioner breaks for the fifth time during the deployment (higher frequency, duration, and intensity), you may notice resentment and anger (toward your spouse or the military). The severity increases, making it more challenging to reframe these thoughts and feelings because they are deeply rooted in the circumstances surrounding the event.

Reaching critical levels of stress is a point at which you may need to reach out or accept help from others.

When stress is ongoing or repeated, with increased frequency and duration, it may be unrealistic to expect yourself to simply reframe negative thoughts about the stress. Reaching critical levels of stress is a point at which you may need to reach out or accept help from others.

If you continually evaluate your thoughts and behaviors, you can begin to naturally notice when they are positive, negative, or neutrally balanced. This is not easy. It takes time and practice, but eventually you will feel empowered to understand your initial response to stress. You will know when and if it is appropriate to focus your thoughts, feelings, and emotions toward a more positive view or to seek outside support.

Trained Beliefs

A hamster wheel keeps turning and turning unless the hamster running it pauses. Our thoughts and emotions operate the same way. Feeling social and emotional stress the same way time after time means we've kept our wheel spinning.

There is a scientific reason why this happens. As we think the same negative thoughts about an event, our brain starts to associate the event with negative emotional and behavioral results. Over time, we learn to train our brains to automatically respond in a negative way. The left brain takes the repeatedly combined thoughts and events and converts them to semipermanent beliefs. These beliefs are then taken from the left brain and formed into permanent attitudes by the right brain.

After continually pairing an event, thought, and feeling, beliefs and attitudes form. Beliefs are the spoken, or conscious, form of attitudes, and once they are formed and stored in the brain, there is no need for the actual event to take place. At this point, words alone can unconsciously trigger the beliefs, which in turn trigger negative emotional and behavioral reactions.

Hidden Attitudes

Your attitudes are like gut beliefs, things you believe so strongly you do not have to think about them before reacting to a situation. They form over time from habitually pairing the same events, thoughts, and feelings. Many of the attitudes you have today were unknowingly formed long ago.

The challenges associated with military life often create unconscious attitudes that extend beyond the time when a spouse is away. Deployments, TDYs, trainings, long hours, weekend obligations, or shift work often require you to function as a single parent. You are left with juggling dinner, laundry piles, soccer practice, violin lessons, and homework on a never-ending list of tasks, perhaps leaving you anxious, depressed, and somewhat resentful. It may happen so often it is hard to remember a time you could depend on your spouse to take on some of the household responsibilities.

These feelings carry through to attitudes post-deployment or after a move. Even if your spouse maintains a normal schedule for several weeks, arrives home early with weekends off, and limits work-related phone calls at home, your attitude of anxiety, depression, or resentment will still be there. Your spouse is now available, but you have learned to associate attitudes based on past experiences when your spouse was not home and available to you and your family.

Attitudes are often triggered by challenges associated with military life, but they are primarily driven by your self-talk. Uncovering underlying attitudes can help you see the situation more clearly and take back control of your behavior through your thoughts and emotions.

To increase your attitude awareness, start by looking at the six main unpleasant feelings of depression, anxiety, anger, guilt, resentment, and hurt. They can stem from irrational underlying attitudes that when challenged, lead to healthier feelings of calm, concern, hope, manageable disappointment, motivation to change, or acknowledged regret.

Depression, or constant sadness, may have underlying attitudes such as "I can't do this," "It's hopeless; nothing will ever change," or even "Military life is awful." Challenge these attitudes. You can do far more than you think and there is always hope in every situation. Military life has many challenges, but there are just as many positive impacts if you choose to look for them.

Anxiety, or excessive worry, may sound like "I would be so worried if my spouse had to deploy or we had to move." Challenge this as well. It would not be terrible if you moved and you are not in physical danger. These possible scenarios may be uncomfortable or new, but nothing bad is happening to you.

Anger is tied to feeling annoyed, displeased, or even hostile toward others. It is often marked with attitudes like "The military shouldn't have," "It's not fair," or even "The military doesn't care about our family." You can accept what has happened and acknowledge that a situation is unfair. If you don't like it, you can take action to change it. Other people and organizations are capable of making mistakes, just like you. Show grace to others the way you would wish they would to you.

Guilt is feeling you have done wrong or failed to do something. It may sound like "I shouldn't have yelled at my spouse for volunteering for a TDY." You chose to take an action, and that action is now finished. Accept responsibility for your actions and use it as an opportunity to motivate you to change.

Resentment or feeling you have been treated unfairly could sound something like, "I shouldn't have to go to all these mandatory military events." Most of the time, no one is forcing you to go to the event. Learning to say "no" is difficult, but powerful. If you say "yes," do it intentionally and with confidence. Only you know your capacity.

Hurt is an expression of mental pain or distress deeply rooted in your expectations. "He didn't come home on time," "She should have called to check in on me," or "They didn't take care of us" are comments based on your perception of what someone should achieve. You will be okay, regardless of others' actions.

Reframed Responses

Changing the way your brain thinks of a situation or anticipates an outcome can be difficult to do on your own. Daily scripts are proven, powerful tools that impose positive thoughts and emotions you may struggle to develop yourself. Pause and take a few deep breaths. Then read aloud each of the following thought shift mantras.

Thought Shift Mantra #1

"What I do does not change me. Sometimes I make mistakes, and sometimes I do things very well, but I'm the same person no matter what I do. Other people have a right to do what they do and to think what they think. Other people's thoughts do not control or define my feelings. I control my thoughts, feelings, and behavior. I feel good about the things I do well and regret some things I do not do well. I accept these behaviors because I accept myself. I feel calm about myself. I feel acceptable to myself. I feel good about accepting myself."

Thought Shift Mantra #2

"I am in control of how I feel. I want to feel calm, and I feel calm now. I am a person worthy of human dignity no matter what other people think of me or how many mistakes I make. I do not need the approval of others to feel calm. Even if people do not think of me the way I would like, I can stand it. I make mistakes like everyone else. I am in control."

Thought Shift Mantra #3

"I may not like what is happening right now, but the world is as it should be. I can do my best and that is good enough. I am responsible for taking action to influence change if I want something to be different. I am calmly reminding myself of my choices as I accept the world as it is now."

By reaffirming calm, concerned, and hopeful thoughts, you refocus negative emotions and see the present moment as it is. Consciously choosing to focus on desirable feelings in your life begins to diminish the power of underlying attitudes and unpleasant feelings. This process cultivates a mindset that is accepting and open, with a choice each day to see the world differently.

> **Reflect:** To identify an underlying attitude, first pinpoint which unpleasant feeling you experience the most. Write it down. Challenge your underlying attitudes by shifting unpleasant feelings to more desirable feelings. Write a new positive version of this feeling. If you are having a hard time writing a positive version, find a scripted mantra or meditation to guide you.

Five Rational Questions

Rational thoughts and behaviors can be difficult to define. What you consider rational may not be rational to others. Rational thoughts can also change over time with situations, age, relationships and many more factors. Five specific questions can help you evaluate if your thoughts are rational or irrational. These questions form the foundation of assessing rational thoughts in each stressful situation.

As you experience a new challenge, ask yourself:

Do my thoughts and behaviors help me feel the way I want to feel?

Rational thoughts and behaviors help you feel the good emotions you want to feel, without alcohol or drugs. Rational thoughts also help protect you from unwanted feelings. Irrational thoughts such as, "I can't get a job because I am not good enough" or "No one wants to hire me; I'll never find a job" could lead to depressed or sad emotions, something you do not want to feel. Rational thoughts such as, "I didn't get this job, but I'm going to start figuring out how to get another job" create hope and motivate you to find a creative solution.

Do my thoughts and behaviors help me protect my well-being?

Rational thoughts and behaviors help protect your life and your health. You want to act on thoughts that keep you healthy and alive. During a lengthy deployment, thoughts such as "I can't stand it; I will never make it through this deployment" or even more significant, "This will never get better" could lead to isolation from friends and family or self-medicating with alcohol or drugs. Neutralizing these irrational thoughts to "I can get through this because I have done it before" or "I'm going to stop making myself feel bad; I'll calmly change what I can" prevents you from self-destructive behaviors.

Do my thoughts and behaviors help me avoid unwanted conflict with others?

Rational thoughts and behaviors help prevent undesirable conflicts or trouble with others. Rational thoughts lead to rational behaviors that ultimately keep you out of conflict. Suppose your coworker failed to meet an important deadline. Thoughts such as, "It's not fair that I always have to pick up extra work" or "I hate that my boss allows this to happen" can lead to arguments with your coworker or boss. A better, more rational thought, would be: "I am confident and know I always do my best work" or "I'm frustrated that this happened again, but I trust my boss will recognize my hard work."

Are my thoughts and behaviors real, based on fact?

Rational thoughts and behaviors are based on obvious facts. If you lie to yourself it makes you feel bad. There is no rational reason to feel bad about the truth. Try using the video camera analogy. Ask yourself: "Would a video camera have recorded the situation exactly as I said it happened?" If the answer is yes, then you probably used facts to describe the situation. However, if the answer is no, then you probably added your opinion to the situation.

Do my thoughts and behaviors help me reach my goals?

Rational thoughts and behaviors help you achieve both your short- and long-term goals. Achieving your goals is more likely to happen when your thoughts support success. Over the past several years, military spouses have started to vigorously tackle entrepreneurship at higher rates. Rational thoughts are a large component of reaching these goals. Spouses who are also entrepreneurs have overcome a multitude of obstacles by telling themselves "This is difficult, but I know it will be worth it in the end" instead of "I will never be able to break through these barriers." Rational thoughts motivate you to move toward your goals.

While it is unrealistic to expect to always answer "yes" for all five questions, answering "yes" to only one or two is usually a good indicator your thoughts or behaviors are irrational. Irrational thoughts and behaviors are common after setbacks from the challenges associated with military life. By continually evaluating your thoughts and behaviors, you will begin to naturally notice when they are rational and irrational. This gives you control over your responses and strengthens your mindset. It is not easy and takes practice, but these five questions are a concrete tool to get you started.

Constructing your thoughts and behaviors to focus on new possibilities will help you face the day-to-day (maybe even minute-to-minute) challenges associated with military life.

Any type of change seems difficult at first. I remember having to change my wake-up time to 4 a.m. when I started a new job. Every morning I wanted to roll over, hit snooze, and wake up at a more reasonable hour. A few weeks into the job, I still could not say I was ecstatic about waking up that early in the morning, but it was a little easier. This is true for any change. At first, it seems difficult, but the more you practice it, the easier it becomes. Like all learning, you need to practice, practice, practice (and offer yourself a little grace along the way) to succeed! Constructing your thoughts and behaviors to focus on new possibilities will help you face the day-to-day (maybe even minute-to-minute) challenges associated with military life.

> **Reflect:** This about a recent stressful situation. Ask yourself the following questions and write down your answers.
>
> ~ What do I want to feel or create in this situation? How can I move toward that outcome?
>
> ~ How can I make the best of this situation?
>
> ~ What can I achieve if I transform my negative thoughts into positive ones?
>
> ~ What new event or thought can I focus on now?
>
> ~ What am I grateful for even in this situation?

Honest vs Pretend Practice

You have the tools, but if you really want to change—and I mean *really* change—you need to practice them intentionally and with honesty, not just pretend to do so. Merely going through the motions is not enough. Honest practice requires action by replacing old beliefs with new attitudes, sincerity, investment, and self-reflection.

Celebrating Transitions

I printed the Honest vs Pretend Practice chart and hung it above my desk. It's a visual reminder that change is hard work, it's intentional, and it's a process. I have used the chart to visualize who I want to be and how I want to show up for others in this exciting but challenging, and sometimes heart-breaking, military journey. That has been important because a sense of ownership, responsibility, and personal power has re-emerged in me that doesn't shy away from but instead celebrates transitions. In letting go of the old behaviors that no longer serve me, I can revel in the excitement and freedom of creating, accepting, and living in a new way of being. —Tiffany L., Air Force spouse

Honest Practice

~ Act in alignment with the behavior you know you want.

~ Replace old beliefs with new ones that are rational for your new behavior.

~ Sincerely intend to make practiced behavior part of your new normal.

~ Use rational thinking to produce new behaviors.

In honest practice, you are primarily interested in how the behavior affects yourself. Genuine learning is taking place.

Pretend Practice

~ Act based on the behavior you *don't* want, with little intention to change.

~ Maintain your old beliefs yet try to get new behavioral results.

~ Do not intend to make a new behavior part of your new normal or you haven't decided or committed yet.

~ Hope new behaviors arrive without changing your thinking to be rational thinking.

In pretend practice, you are primarily interested in how your behavior affects someone else instead of how it affects you. Genuine learning is not *taking place.*

Reflect: After reading these characteristics, you should have insight into whether you believe you are being honest with yourself. Are you improving your emotional well-being or just pretending?

Being a rational thinker and doer will help you no matter what stage of life you are in. As a military spouse, learning how to think, feel, and act rationally will continue to serve you long after your military tenure is over. This is not a quick fix. Just as eating better and becoming more active contributes to a healthier body, the skills you gain by practicing these techniques will result in a new emotionally healthy way of life for you and your entire family.

Chapter Reflection

~ Note your thoughts about the three thought paths. How do you believe you have responded to stress in the past (positive, neutral, or negative)?

~ Recall a stressful event. Detail the experience in terms of what actually happened, your perception of the event, immediate thoughts and emotions you felt, and what behaviors you showed as a result.

Event:

Perception:

Thoughts:

Emotions:

Behavior:

~ Look at the thoughts, emotions, and behaviors you listed. Circle positive thoughts, emotions, and behaviors. Draw a line through negative ones. Leave the neutral ones.

~ Think back to a time when you believe your stress was at critical levels (increased frequency, duration, and/or intensity). How did you respond?

~ After reading through "hidden attitudes," can you identify any you may have? Why do you believe these hidden attitudes have formed? What can you do to challenge them?

~ What unpleasant feeling (depression, anxiety, anger, guilt, resentment, hurt) do you experience the most after a stressful situation? Now think about the feeling you desire in that situation (calm, concern, hope, manageable disappointment, motivation to change, acknowledged regret). Every time you feel the unpleasant feeling, imagine the more pleasant one.

~ Look back at the negative thoughts, emotions, and behaviors you noted. Using the five questions strategy, evaluate any areas where they do not make you feel the way you want to, support your well-being, avoid conflict with others, present reality based on facts, or help you attain your goals. Write down examples of how you can shift thoughts that do not support the five areas into more neutral or positive ones.

~ Are you practicing change honestly or pretending to do so? What steps can you take to improve honest practice of your response to stress?

CHAPTER 4

Manage

Give Permission to Pause

*We often save the best version of ourselves for spouses,
children, and friends—try adding yourself to the top of the list.*

EACH DAY AS I ENTERED THE GARAGE to get in my car to drive
to work, I wondered how we managed to fill a three-car garage with
so much stuff. I challenged my husband one day and asked him, "Do
you seriously need all of these tools?" His response, shocked at the
horror of such a question, was that each one has a specific use and
purpose. He had to keep them all just in case the opportunity arose
where we needed a particular tool. Tools to manage stress can be
viewed in much the same way.

At this point in your journey of learning about stress, you
have noted stress you may be experiencing, gained insight into the
potential effects, and analyzed your response through thoughts,
feelings, and emotions. Now it is useful to look at what tools you need
to manage your stress. Sometimes stress feels momentous like going
through a deployment, or ridiculous like daily arguments with your
teenage daughter, but you can get stuck by it either way. When you're
stuck, managing stress is a kind of psychological trick you can learn
as a way to cope with what otherwise might seem impossible.

The goal of getting unstuck is not to solve the problem of stress,
but rather to acquire tools to manage it now and in the future. Much
like the tools cluttering a garage, your toolkit will be overflowing
once you understand the specific use each technique serves. And you
will be able to pull out the tool you need for the situation you face.
Through better management of stress, you can begin to experience
challenges as growth opportunities without suffering. It makes a
simple, yet profound difference.

Resiliency

Resiliency, a person's ability to bounce back from a jarring setback, has evolved into an attractive term used often in the military. We hear it used to describe the twelve-year-old military child who has been in four different elementary schools or the spouse who has endured five deployments while running a home business.

> *The goal of getting unstuck is not to solve the problem of stress, but rather to acquire tools to manage it now and in the future.*

While resiliency may be easy to define, it is much more difficult to achieve. Many of the challenges faced by military families are intense and of long duration. Military spouses face unique challenges over extended periods of time and are often praised for being resilient and strong, but there is a disconnect between social and personal resiliency. This disconnect places extremely high expectations, and often increased pressure, on spouses to always be resilient. We may not always feel resilient, but this external expectation prevents us from owning up to the truth.

A personal experience of this pressure started during our first year in North Carolina. There were several formal and informal events within the unit, some my husband and I attended together, but many I attended alone due to his deployments. During one particular promotional event, a senior officer recounted the highlights of an officer's career by culminating his speech with genuine praise for the promotee's supportive wife. This respected spouse was well cherished within the military community for her countless volunteer hours planning successful events for military spouses. The speaker looked directly at the wife and, with warm sincerity, firmly stated she truly was the "epitome of a Spartan wife" (I later learned this is a very common reference used to describe military spouses in Special Operations). The audience shook their heads up and down, nodding in approval, but it struck a personal nerve. Reacting to the association between military spouses and Spartan women, I became concerned that military spouses were expected to be by definition "disciplined, powerful, and threatening."

I knew at that time I was different from the woman he praised. I felt powerless and seemingly lacked control of almost everything. I wasn't even sure I was capable of tackling the daily demands of military life without my husband. Yes, I knew military spouses are absolutely capable of Spartan performance and we all embody and interpret Spartan capabilities in different ways, but the label left little room for admitting "I'm not okay." Resiliency first requires us to pause and recognize the setback or stress we are experiencing and then a positive approach to responding to it.

Adopting a positive mindset is similar to a flight attendant's plea to put on your own oxygen mask before helping others. When you honor the importance of restoration and strengthening tools for yourself, it benefits others too. The real impact of that supportive wife was her ability to care for others because she had taken care of herself first. We have no way of avoiding stress entirely, but we can take proactive steps to protect ourselves from suffering.

Restoration

Restoration, or self-care, is the process of recovering after damage. It is essential not only when working through difficult situations, but also when learning new tools to manage stress. You will be uncomfortable at times, but real change takes place when you stay patient and committed. Whether you have one free minute or thirty in your day, self-care is possible and worth it.

To intentionally make self-care part of your daily routine, begin by noting the time of day that is best for your self-care. What time in your day could you benefit most from a mental break? When do you usually feel stressed and could use a reset? Is there a time of day that would help you positively approach situations that typically feel stressful to you? With 1,440 minutes in every day, you have a vast window of opportunity.

Determine how much time you realistically have for your self-care at that time of day: one minute, five minutes, or thirty minutes. Recall from chapter one the four areas that stress can affect: physical, emotional, cognitive, and behavioral. Restoration involves building specific tools for each of these areas to better manage stress.

Physical Restoration Tools

Getting immunizations, taking vitamins, and receiving annual checkups with doctors all are routine actions we take to avoid sickness and remain physically healthy. We value physical health because of the known impact if we do not. Stress, much like a bacteria or virus, can have similar physical effects: lack of energy, insomnia or hypersomnia, aches, pains, or muscle tension, just to name a few. Adding regular tools to address the physical effects of stress can be your daily mental health vitamin for the future.

One Minute

There are many functions of modern smartwatches to love, with quick access to texts, phone calls, or emails. One hidden perk is breathing applications that randomly prompt the user to consciously take slow, controlled breaths.

Deep breathing, even for a minute, can slow down your heart rate. It allows your body to take in more oxygen and signals the brain to wind down, balancing your hormones. Just as stress increases cortisol levels, deep breathing lowers them and increases endorphins to the body. Endorphins, otherwise known as the feel-good hormone, can alleviate depression, reduce anxiety, boost self-esteem, and even improve your immune system.

Fortunately, you do not need a smartwatch to prompt and guide you through deep breathing. The instant breathing maneuver is simple, takes about a minute, and is ideally performed five times a day. You can practice breathing anywhere, even while waiting in line.

Instant Breathing Maneuver

~ Find a quiet, comfortable place

~ Close your eyes

~ Inhale and exhale deeply and slowly, expanding your belly

~ Hold your breath and relax for three to four seconds

~ Repeat the sequence for one to five minutes

Fifteen Minutes

After a long day, you may notice tightness in your shoulders, back, or legs—a common physiological response to stress. Progressive muscle relaxation, or PMR, is a common technique to reduce this muscle tension. Its effectiveness comes from slowly tensing and releasing all the major muscles in your system from your head to your feet. Relaxing the muscles in your body can minimize your stress reactivity and decrease your experience of chronic stress.

Progressive Muscle Relaxation

~ Find a quiet place and sit or lie down, whichever is more comfortable. Unfold your arms and uncross your legs so you have easy circulation and your body can relax.

~ Begin by tensing the muscles in your face and scalp. Make a tight grimace, close your eyes as tightly as possible, clench your teeth, even move your ears up if you can. Hold this for the count of eight as you inhale. Now exhale and relax completely, as though you are sleeping. Feel the tension seep from your facial muscles and enjoy the feeling. Take your time and relax completely before you move onto the next step.

~ Next, completely tense your neck and shoulders, again inhaling and counting to eight. Then exhale and relax. This step can be repeated until you feel absolutely relaxed in this area, particularly because many people carry tension in their neck and shoulder muscles. Take your time and let your tension go.

~ Continue down your body, repeating the procedure with the following muscle groups: chest, abdomen, right arm, right forearm, right hand (making a fist), left arm, left forearm, left hand, buttocks, upper right leg, lower right leg, right foot, upper left leg, lower left leg, left foot.

~ For a shortened version, combine and focus on four main muscle groups: face; neck, shoulders, and arms; abdomen and chest; and buttocks, legs, and feet.

Although PMR is a tool that can be performed at any time, it is especially useful when trying to go to sleep. With practice, you can relax your body as if 'liquid relaxation' is being poured on your head and flowing down to your toes.

Thirty Minutes

Move your body. Exercise increases the concentration of brain chemicals that regulate stress levels and produce feel-good endorphins. As a side benefit, it increases your physical fitness which can improve self-worth and self-image.

Select a physical activity you know you can incorporate as a regular part of your daily routine. Self-care should be treated like practice and is not a quick fix. Throwing on a pair of running shoes for the first time in months and trying to complete a 5K race is probably not realistic.

A thirty-minute walk is a great example of an achievable goal. As the most inexpensive, accessible, and low-risk form of exercise, walking can be performed almost anytime, anywhere, and at your own pace. Studies have revealed that walking thirty minutes can be the equivalent of a sleeping pill for those who struggle with insomnia. Many doctors informally call a thirty-minute walk the most under-utilized stress buster.

For military spouses who have a physical disability or other barrier to walking, alternative techniques such as chair yoga, water aerobics, or stationary bicycling, also work quite well.

Emotional Restoration Tools

Stress can often create a flood of emotions, arriving all at once and making it difficult to control. Overwhelming sadness, fatigue, persistent worry, or being irritated with seemingly inconsequential events are common examples of the way stress influences emotion. The emotional effects of stress can be profound. Learning tools to cope with these emotions can better manage your overall stress.

Just like the tools for addressing physical aspects of stress, the tools for emotional stress can be tailored to the amount of available time you have, whether it is one minute or thirty.

One Minute

Gratitude lists or journals have flooded the market of positive psychology and for good reason. This common tool helps focus attention on the positive aspects of your life, eliciting more positive emotions, which can improve your stress response. According to the growing body of research on positive psychology, gratitude journals contribute to decreased signs of depression, heart disease, and stress, as well as to improved interpersonal relationships.

> **Gratitude Journal**
>
> ~ Select a time of day with minimal interruptions.
>
> ~ Find a dedicated notebook or journal.
>
> ~ Place a date at the top of each page (this is great data to reflect on over time).
>
> ~ Write down five events from your day (or the previous day if you write in the morning) that you were grateful for.

Another successful variation of a gratitude journal is an accomplishment journal. In the same fashion, write down five things you accomplished that day (or a previous day). It does not have to be a massive or profound accomplishment, such as tackling every box in your house post-move. It might be as simple as noting you showered that day, fed your children, and went to bed on time. Again, this technique strengthens your focus on what you did instead of did not. There is no right way to create or engage with a gratitude journal. Find what works best for you.

Fifteen Minutes

Unfortunately, gratitude journals have a potential pitfall—they are not always effective if you just go through the motions of writing on the paper. You also have to believe in your gratitude. You can increase the effectiveness of this tool by expanding on the experience. This involves being intentional about your list and reflecting on the items you write about.

Expanded Gratitude Journal

~ Take your list of five events or accomplishments you are grateful for and elaborate in detail about the aspects that made you feel grateful.

~ Who was there? Focus on the people that made you feel grateful instead of the things.

~ Try subtraction, not just addition. Reflect on what your life would be like without certain blessings. Appreciate what you have today.

~ Note any surprising experiences, especially if things worked out better than you expected or hoped. This can strengthen your level of gratitude.

Thirty Minutes

Suppose you finish your first half-marathon. As you cross the finish line, a feeling of exhaustion overwhelms you. You do not feel the underlying contentment or tranquility of the moment because you are far too tired. Later, as you reflect on the race, you realize how joyful and satisfying it was to finish the race. You wish you had noticed those feelings more in the moment instead of the exhaustion. Very strong emotions, such as when you are upset, frightened, or even extremely happy, inhibit the ability to pay attention to weaker, but still meaningful, emotions. This effect is known as emotional escalation. Combating the effects of emotional escalation starts by practicing grounding techniques, turning your attention away from thoughts, memories, or worries, and refocusing on the present moment. One such grounding technique is an immediate five sense activity. The goal is to notice small details that your mind typically tunes out. With practice, this technique can be added to your toolkit to help you stay calm, feel content, and stay present to prevent emotional escalation.

Immediate Five Senses Activity

~ Select a notebook and a comfortable space.

~ Write down five things you can see. Look for small details such as the pattern on tiles in your office, the way the light reflects in your kitchen, or an object you never noticed before.

~ Write down four things you can feel. Notice the sensation of the shirt on your body, the sun on your skin, or the feeling of the couch you are sitting on. You can also pick up an object and note the weight, texture, and other physical qualities.

~ Write down three things you hear. Pay close attention to the sounds your mind magically turns out, such as the hum of the refrigerator, traffic outside your home, or the wind blowing through trees.

~ Write down two things you smell. Try to notice smells in the air around you, like the candle burning in your bathroom, a flower, or the newly mowed grass.

~ Write down one thing you can taste. Pick up your favorite snack or drink for this step. Take a bite or sip and focus your attention on the complex flavors you can taste.

Cognitive Restoration Tools

As a society we tend to hyper-focus on our body and emotions because signs of change are more obvious—both positive and negative. However, taking care of your mind is just as important. Recall the potential cognitive effects of stress: lack of focus, a hard time making decisions, forgetfulness, or disorganization. These effects, if gone unaddressed, can impact your ability to function just as much if not more than the physical manifestations of stress.

One Minute

Mental exercises can help take your mind off uncomfortable thoughts and feelings. They are discreet and can be done at any place or time. An added bonus of mental exercises is they increase your focus, boost brain power, and decrease anxiety and depression. Imagine this exercise like a gymnastics routine for your brain:

Mental Gymnastics

~ Name all the objects you see in the room.

~ Describe the steps of performing an activity you know well, such as preparing your favorite recipe, driving a car, or folding laundry.

~ Count backward by sevens, starting at one hundred.

~ Spell your full name and the names of three people you know, backward.

~ Name all your family members, their ages, and one of their favorite foods.

~ Think of an object and draw it in your mind. Try drawing your pet, car, or bedroom. If you are feeling adventurous, try drawing it upside down.

For another quick mental exercise tool, add music! Listen to happy music while preparing dinner or getting ready for work. Happy tunes have been shown to boost creative thinking and brainpower. Crank up your favorite feel-good music.

Fifteen Minutes

Guided imagery, when done intentionally, can change your brain's cognitive processing of stressful events. Through repeated practice, you can reduce the grey matter in the brain's amygdala (the region associated with stress), increase the grey matter in the prefrontal cortex (the region associated with planning and problem solving), and promote a thicker hippocampus (responsible for memory and learning).

Though guided imagery is a rather cumbersome title, it is a simple technique that can quickly calm your body and relax your mind. It both reduces current stress and prepares you for future stress. There are many ways to practice guided imagery. You can seek out guided imagery instructors in your community, find audio or video recordings online, or perform the practice entirely on your own! You follow the same steps in a guided video as you do using your inner voice and imagination, it is simply a personal preference.

Guided Imagery

~ Sit on a cushion, lie down, or find another comfortable position.

~ Start taking deep breaths to relax your body.

~ Once you get to a relaxed state, begin to envision yourself in the most relaxing environment you can imagine. For some, this would be floating in the cool, clear waters off a remote tropical island, where soft music plays in the background and waves crash against the sand. For others, it might be sitting by a campfire surrounded by snow, sipping coffee, and reading a favorite book.

~ Involve your senses: Can you hear the ocean waves, taste the salty water, feel the warm sun on your face, or see the palm trees waving in the wind?

~ Relax: Stay here for as long as you like. Enjoy the environment you have created and let yourself be far from what stresses you. When you are ready, count back from twenty, and tell yourself when you get to "one" you'll feel calm and alert. You'll feel refreshed, like returning from a mini vacation, but you won't need to physically leave the room!

Tips to improve your experience:

~ Try using ambient sounds that compliment your imagery. This can help you feel more immersed in your environment, or help drown out the sounds of real-life surroundings.

~ Set an alarm. Guided imagery is a relaxing technique so don't be surprised if you fall asleep or lose track of time. If you set an alarm, you will be more prone to relax and let go.

Thirty Minutes

Recall from chapter three the importance of differentiating between rational and irrational thoughts. You were given basic tools to help identify the differences between the two, but you can further develop your awareness by going through rational self-analysis, also known as a rational thinking journal. This activity walks you through a stressful event and asks you to challenge thoughts, feelings, and behaviors which may or may not be irrational. By doing this, you can further strengthen your ability to cognitively reframe your responses to stress.

Rational Thinking Journal

~ Pick a dedicated notebook (or computer file) for this journal.

~ Divide the paper into two columns.

~ Label the left side "Initial Approach" and the right side "Rational Approach."

~ Under each column, write: Event, Perception, Thoughts, Emotions, and Behavior

~ Go to the Initial Approach side of the paper.

~ Under Event, list any details you recall about the stressful experience.

~ For Perception, recall what you noticed with your senses.

~ Write the initial thoughts you remember having in the moment under Thoughts.

~ Describe your feelings that followed under Emotions.

~ Under Behavior, write down the result. What happened? How did you respond?

~ Now go to the Rational Approach side of the paper.

~ Pretend you are viewing the event through a camera lens, as if a picture were taken. Write down under Event exactly what you would see through this lens.

~ Review your initial perception. What other sensory details could you have noticed that may change your perception?

~ Review your initial thoughts. Were they positive, negative, or neutral (based on the five criteria)? If they were negative or neutral, challenge them by writing down a positive thought.

~ Review your emotions from your initial response. Were these feelings you wanted to have? If not, write down your desired emotions under the rational side.

~ Review your initial behavior. Were your actions or results what you wanted? If not, write down your desired actions or behaviors under the rational side.

Initial Approach	Rational Approach
Event:	Event:
Perception:	Perception:
Thoughts:	Thoughts:
Emotions:	Emotions:
Behavior:	Behavior:

Behavioral Restoration Tools

Have you ever gone to bed thinking the next day will be a repeat of your last? As creatures of habit, we typically do many of the same things, in the same way, every day. The body and mind become accustomed to the same pattern. This makes behavioral change much more difficult, yet also far more rewarding. It is an opportunity to take a risk and reap the benefits of improved social and emotional well-being.

One Minute

A quick behavioral change means changing a small element of your daily routine. It is easy to get stuck in a rut when it comes to daily tasks. Try new ways of doing the same things. For example, if you drive the same way to work every day, try a different route to work. Or switch the type of transportation. If you normally drive, could you bike or walk? Even if you take the same route, you could listen to different music on the ride or dance for a minute when you get out of the car. Another application is shifting your exercise routine from running each morning to lifting weights every other day. Simple behavioral changes do not take much additional time, if any, but doing so creates benefits for you by stimulating the brain and releasing more positive endorphins.

Fifteen Minutes

Are you one of the three in ten adults who do not get enough sleep? Tackling sleep issues can be difficult, but extremely important. Being able to fall into a deep sleep can reboot your body. Research has shown that getting enough sleep every night can help you recover from a physical illness and decrease emotional fatigue. To learn what could potentially be keeping you up at night and robbing you of good night's sleep, start a two-week journal on your behavioral sleep patterns. It takes about fifteen minutes per day and you will likely be surprised at what you learn.

Sleep Journal

For two weeks, write down the following details in a journal:

~ What you did thirty minutes before bed

~ What time you went to bed

~ What time you fell asleep, if known

~ How many times you woke up during the night

~ How long it took you to fall back asleep each time you woke up

~ The time you woke up in the morning

~ How many naps you took during the day, and for how long

~ Any medications you take

~ Your caffeine or alcohol intake in the three hours before bed

Depending on what you discover in your sleep journal, here are some tips to consider:

- Avoid checking emails or texts thirty minutes before bed. The blue light from the screen keeps your brain from releasing melatonin, the hormone that aids in sleep. Read a good book, listen to music, or have a cup of tea.
- Exercise, but do it at the right time. Consistent exercise helps promote deep sleep, but doing it right before bed can be counterproductive.
- Try to get at least seven hours of sleep every night. Banking sleep hours on the weekend while skimping during the week is not effective.
- Go to bed and get up at the same time every day. Keeping to the same sleep schedule will help regulate your body's sleep patterns.
- Alcohol is not helpful for sleep. It can make you feel relaxed but it also prevents you from getting deep sleep, the kind that restores your body.
- Check your medications. Some medications are known to have more caffeine than an eight-ounce cup of coffee and could be preventing you from falling asleep.

Thirty Minutes

Behavioral activation is a method in which you identify specific goals for the week and work toward meeting those goals. The goals could be activities you enjoy doing. For example, if you want to work toward being a more compassionate person, you could choose goals that center on volunteering, helping out another military spouse, or donating time to your favorite charity for thirty minutes each day. This technique is designed to increase your contact with both positive and rewarding experiences. Positive behavior can positively affect your mood.

> **Reflect:** Take a look at your schedule and determine where you have time for self-care. Is it in the morning when you first wake up, in the afternoon, or right before bed? Don't see a gap? Make one. Put self-care on your list of most important appointments. How much time do you have at that time of day? Which of the physical, emotional, cognitive, and behavioral restoration tools resonated most with you? Put them on your calendar.

Strengthening

After running for several weeks, you might feel a desire to increase your mileage or go for a more challenging run. Strengthening or enriching the management of stress is similar to this experience. You start small with a few restoration techniques and eventually seek out opportunities to build stronger tools to manage stress. Today, you might be comfortable with your current mileage and wait to strengthen your stress management. That is okay too! Whether you are ready to go down this path today or in the future, the tools will be available for you when you need them.

Goal Setting

Write down a goal you want to achieve, such as eat more vegetables, sleep longer, or exercise more frequently. Be specific. The more details you outline about the goal, the more likely you are to succeed. For example, suppose your goal is to exercise more frequently. Outline this goal with specific details about what you want to achieve, noting the frequency (how often), duration (how long), and any measures you will take to keep yourself accountable.

Goal: **Exercise More Frequently**

What: Write down the type of exercise, such as walking, running, weight lifting, yoga, or a combination. Pick something you enjoy.

Frequency: Indicate how often you will exercise. Circle the days you plan to exercise on your calendar.

Duration: Pick the time of day and how long you will exercise. Go back to the calendar and under the days you circled, block out the exact time you plan to exercise.

Location: Within the block of time, write in where you will exercise and what activity you will perform. For example, run two miles in the neighborhood or lift weights at the base gym.

Accountability: Within your plan, note how you will be held accountable. Incorporating friends or workout partners can help, but can also hinder your progress if the person often cancels. Track on your calendar the days you were successful and note the days you were not. Be detailed when you could not complete the goal. Was it lack of time, preparation, or something else? Try to remove those barriers for next time.

Reward: Select a weekly reward. Fridays could be your cheat days where you relax and binge watch your favorite TV or streaming series. Give yourself the grace to enjoy a day off from your goal as it will increase the likelihood of you moving forward.

Ask For Advice: There is no reason to try to face challenges all on your own. Ask friends or family members for ideas or solutions that have (or have not) worked for them in the past. This also helps with accountability, as that person may become invested in your journey.

Learned Resourcefulness

Navigating your way through challenges and growing from stress is not just an individual journey. Military spouses who use the support of friends, family, and trusted professionals to help them achieve their goals are much more likely to succeed in developing tools to strengthen from stress. Psychologists use the term "learned resourcefulness" to describe the way we grow stronger from working together. It is significantly different from resiliency. Resiliency refers to our individual ability to recover from stressful situations, whereas learned resourcefulness refers to what we are capable of as military spouses collectively.

Your fellow military spouses are your own best resource! Researchers have found repeatedly that social support is one of the strongest tools designed to help military families. You can become stronger together because of your common experiences. When you share your story with those around you, it helps others learn and grow, in addition to helping you create connections and avoid feeling alone or isolated. For example, if one spouse shares the struggle of finding a good school in a new area, others will likely relate to that experience, creating a community of people and resources who share a similar struggle.

Social connections also strengthen emotional well-being. As you build community in a new area, consider sharing your thoughts and feelings with those around you on your journey. For example, you might share your gratitude journal (or messages you learned from it) with friends, neighbors, or family. This helps them better understand your goals and how they can support you. It can also help you remain accountable to yourself and your goals.

Helping You Helped Me

The first time I heard the statistics about military spouse stress, honestly, I was surprised by the magnitude of the stress and how it didn't matter how old you are or what rank the service member is. It really challenged my point of view and caused me to re-evaluate my behavior. Since hearing about military spouse stress and the impact it has on so many people, I've been more attentive, more compassionate, and more forgiving, particularly with myself. I am more willing to talk about the stress I feel. I now give myself latitude to take breaks and to take care of myself so I can take better care of others. I also found that by acknowledging the stress, I became more relatable and approachable. I was very thankful for the information. Now I'm more involved in helping alleviate some of that stress for others, and in the process, it alleviates some of mine. —Kendra G., Air Force spouse

If sharing your thoughts, emotions, and feelings with others is intimidating, that's okay. It isn't easy to be vulnerable and open up. When you are ready, helping others can help you.

Take a risk. Start a book club, weekly coffee, or walking group. Social connection can strengthen your ability to move through or past stressful events. Military spouses can support each other. We are stronger together! By using that collective strength, it can not only reinforce individual self-care skills but also create an environment for more positive stress experiences.

Thieves

Do you often wake up with motivation to conquer the day, only to feel disappointed at the end of the day when only two or three items got crossed off the to-do list? The time and energy of the day seem to have vanished after getting caught up in lots of distractions. I like to imagine this situation as little "thieves" stealing from you throughout the day while you are not paying attention. Sometimes these thieves can be so much a part of your life that you stopped realizing their impact long ago. Two of the most common examples of these distractions are time thieves and emotional thieves.

Time Thieves

When you are not as productive as you want to be, it can seem like time passed too quickly or the day did not hold the usual number of hours. Productivity might be fairly easy to measure in some workplaces, where you can say you knocked out five reports or gave two presentations, but it can be quite challenging to measure in military life. You often find yourself surrounded by unexpected situations that suck up massive chunks of time. You are left thinking, "What *did* happen today?" Recognizing five common hidden time stealers can help you maintain goals, strengthen confidence, and move forward.

Distractions

Distractions are everywhere in our lives. Like stress, they can be both internal (thoughts and habits) or external (environmental and relationships). It is hard to get things done in a constant state of distraction, leaving you upset that you only unpacked one box or received ten new emails while you were working on something else. Set clear boundaries with family and friends, and check in with your internal thoughts so you can focus your attention where you want it.

Overscheduling

In my experience, I have found that military spouses are not exceptionally skilled at saying "no." Suppose you have a standing Tuesday lunch with a friend following a car repair appointment and as your meal is delivered, your spouse calls to see if you can attend the booster club meeting. You want to support your spouse (and unit), but there is power in saying no. Before you make a decision, consider that every additional commitment you accept must be balanced with something else on your plate. When you say yes, you either need to drop an equivalent promise or try to find more time for the new one. You may not have free time to add responsibilities if you are already working at your maximum.

Phone Interruptions

The buzzing phone is a notorious time thief. The average individual gets interrupted by their phone every eleven minutes, and research has shown it can take up to twenty-five minutes to return to a task. Ask yourself if you need to instantly respond or whether that call, text, or email reply can wait. Try muting your phone for a set time every day if you know you need to stay focused. Turn off your notifications for non-emergency uses while working on projects.

Social Media

A related thief is excessive social media use. Scrolling through a feed can lead to following links to articles, shopping the ad that pops up, or any number of other time-consuming distractions.

In today's world, we rely heavily on social media for connection. As military families, with friends and family distributed across the world, this reality is even more true. We also use it to find new friends and groups, seek emotional support, or discover new resources in our community. However, viewing others' pictures and posts can also leave you feeling isolated or insecure about your life. You could develop a fear of missing out, thinking that others are having more fun or enjoying their life more than you. Excessive social media use can increase feelings of isolation, depression, and anxiety. I consider social media a time thief rather than an emotional one since, in addition to the scrolling, the time we spend feeling sorry for ourselves or developing insecurities is time that would be better spent on other things.

Procrastination

Procrastination is one of the most common time thieves we create for ourselves. The move will come in three months, whether you accept it or not. Waiting until the last minute to prepare for many of the challenges associated with military life will leave you anxious and unprepared. Make a list and try to tackle something on it every day. Prioritize your well-being and take proactive steps to end each day feeling accomplished, which will decrease your internal stress.

Emotional Thieves

Building social connections with friends, family, and community members can help you, but only in moderation. Do not be afraid to turn down an opportunity if it is not right for you at the time.

"You know what you signed up for" or "You know what you need to do to get through this deployment" are comments most military spouses have heard at some point in their tenure, and they can leave you feeling put down, anxious, sad, or even depressed. You hear these comments and commit to screening the next phone call or try to avoid seeing that person. Know the signs of these three common personalities that cause additional stress—taking away opportunities for you to strengthen and grow:

Narcissist

A person with a narcissistic personality claims to have the perfect solution to all your problems: spending more time and energy with them. They lack empathy or understanding, and their love is often conditional. It is all about them and can be frustrating. Try to maintain realistic expectations of this person and never make your self-worth contingent on them.

Victim

Someone with a victim mentality circles all of your struggles back to their own. They maintain a sense that the world is against them and their struggles are more significant than those of others, often dominating the conversation. It can be draining as you inevitably end up trying to support them instead of seeking support for yourself. Try to set boundaries: "I love you but I only have five minutes right now."

Controller

A controller is obsessed with trying to control and dictate how you are supposed to be or feel. They invalidate your experiences and leave you feeling dominated, demeaned, or put down. The secret to this individual: don't try to control the controller. Try saying: "I value your input, but I need to work through this myself."

Individuals like these are not always pleasant to interact with, but are important to recognize as they can negatively influence your emotional responses and behaviors. If you find yourself exhibiting some of the same traits as these personalities, consider how you can improve your response to others going through challenging situations. There is much to learn by watching and observing others. Take inventory of events and people who fill you up or take away your energy. Try to focus your time and surround yourself with loving, nurturing people on your journey.

Milspouse Strength ~ Kendra Lowe

Resources

There are many forms of support designed to ensure military family stability. Since the September 11, 2001 terrorist attacks, numerous programs have been developed to help meet the needs of contemporary military families. These programs take place at various levels, including special military commands, military communities, and the Department of Defense.

One program implemented by the United States Special Operations Command is called Preservation of the Force and Family (POTFF). The mission of the POTFF initiative is "to identify and implement innovative, valuable solutions ... aimed at improving the short- and long-term well-being of our Special Operations Forces (SOF) warriors and their families."

> *I attended a POTFF-funded program while in North Carolina. It provided a weekend retreat, complete with childcare and chaplain services, to help with the reintegration process after my husband's return from a long deployment. I found myself depressed post-deployment and thought I was crazy for it. Who wouldn't be thrilled to have their husband home? But I realized that weekend that I was dealing with so much more than just the deployment. —Sarah N., Air Force spouse*

Another initiative called Families Overcoming Under Stress (FOCUS) was created by the University of California, Los Angeles (UCLA) and the Harvard School of Medicine. This prevention program was specially developed for military families at Camp Pendleton. It teaches families how to cope with separation, routine shifts, and fear of loss of the service member, as well as the physical and psychological stress experienced by service members. This comprehensive program was developed to teach resiliency skills to service members, dependent spouses, and their children.

> *My husband has been a Marine for fifteen years. I wondered what they [FOCUS] could possibly tell me that I don't already know. I was surprised by all the information we actually used. —Marine Corps Spouse*

At the national level, communities have developed several associations, such as the National Military Family Association (NMFA) and the Military Child Education Coalition (MCEC), aimed at supporting military families. The American Psychological Association (APA) developed the Task Force on Military Deployment Services for Youth, Families, and Service Members. This APA program is aimed at helping professional psychologists recognize and respond to the unique needs of military families. Yet another program, called Coming Together Around Military Families (CTAMF), provides professional training, consultations, and materials to military families in more than sixty-five communities.

The Department of Defense has also emphasized the challenges associated with reintegration and initiated a program called Strong Families. This home-based parenting program contains eight intervention modules designed to help military families during critical periods. Strong Families pays increased attention to deployment stress (child separation and service member mental health problems), parent-child relationships, and parenting stress during reintegration that is critical within the military community.

Another program aimed at meeting the needs of military families is the Military and Family Life Counseling Program (MFLC). The MFLC Program trains consultants to counsel military families on relationships, crisis intervention, stress management, grief, occupational, and other special and family-related issues. This program, unlike other military support programs, provides a Child and Youth Program (CYP), which is integrated into school systems to explicitly help military children.

Can I Keep My MFLC?

I was so excited to finally find a counselor I liked! My friend had recently recommended a new MFLC assigned to our husband's group, and she told me she really liked her, so I thought I would give it a try. I was skeptical at first because I had gone to counselors before and just didn't make a connection. Well, maybe that's not completely true. I did find one who was amazing three years ago, but then we had to move. And I didn't make the effort to find another one—probably because I thought I didn't need one anymore.

But three years later, I found myself struggling with the same issues. I didn't feel like I had an identity in the Army separate from my husband, and I wanted to find a way to be happier with myself. So I was excited to get a personal recommendation of a counselor who worked well with military spouses—not to mention I knew MFLCs did not take notes, and there was a certain comfort that came with that fact. I called to schedule my first meeting, and she actually recommended we meet for coffee for the first time to get to know each other. I didn't know that MFLCs could meet with spouses outside their offices. We hit it off immediately. —Michelle G., Army spouse

While this resource list is by no means exhaustive, it highlights available resources for you and your family. However, even with all these resources, many families do not get the support they need and resources go underutilized as a result of mental health stigmas.

Mental Health Stigma

There are several harmful stigmas about mental health that prevent some spouses or active duty service members from reaching out for help. Although these stigmas have been decreasing over time, they remain embedded within the military community.

It is common for military spouses to worry about notes or records being taken, tracked, and possibly reported from conversations they have with professionals. They sometimes hesitate to seek mental health support because of a perceived potential negative impact on their service member's career or military clearance.

Active duty service members commonly express concerns that receiving psychological services and treatment could be perceived as weakness, that units or squadrons would have less confidence in them, or that their chain of command will treat them differently.

These thoughts are not surprising since military veterans and families have long been taught to harbor negative attitudes toward mental health treatment through their years of service. But the continuation of these stigmas remains concerning.

There is a significant need for military spouses to have access to professionals who are not only trained to provide effective interventions, but who also understand the unique stress associated with military life. Negative beliefs associated with the need for clinical care undoubtedly influence how military members and their families respond to a range of educational and mental health professionals. Whether you are currently experiencing severe stress or are learning about it for the first time, it is always better to seek help if you think you need it.

While seeking help is important, choosing the right resource to get that help is equally vital. Not all professional resources are created equal, and resources span a vast spectrum in both levels of service and confidentiality. For example, MFLCs provide non-medical counseling and therefore are not required to take notes, while psychiatrists have the ability to prescribe medications and will have to document. There are resources available, both military and civilian, based on your needs. You can help tackle the mental health stigma by using these resources when you need them and advocating for others to do the same.

As military spouses, we often save the best version of ourselves for spouses, children, or friends—let this be a reminder that adding yourself to the list is just as important. Effective management of your stress can break you out of emotional gridlock and strengthen your well-being. By applying these tools, you will not only be better prepared to manage stress today, but also long into the future.

Chapter Reflection

~ Do you take time for yourself each day and week? If yes, write down what you do and how you feel afterward. If not, write down why you believe it is important to practice self-care moving forward.

~ How much time can you commit each day to your self-care: one minute, fifteen minutes, or thirty minutes? How you will prioritize this time in your schedule?

~ Try a physical, cognitive, emotional, or behavioral technique within your dedicated time. What did you notice about this experience? How did you feel afterward? Discuss your experience with your spouse, trusted friend, or support group.

~ Where is goal setting most effective in your life? If you often struggle to meet your goals, consider if they are realistic and evaluate anything that may be preventing you from achieving them.

~ What were your thoughts on reading about learned resourcefulness? How have you connected with military spouses in the past and what can you do to better connect with military spouses for future support?

~ Did you identify with any time thieves or emotional thieves? What can you do to remove these distractions?

~ What mental health resources have been most effective for you during your time as a military spouse? Are there new resources you want to learn more about?

~ Note your experiences with the mental health stigma in our military culture. What can you do to help promote positive mental health attitudes?

CHAPTER 5

Grow

Learn to Prepare

Military life is your teacher;
your challenge is to be the student.

MY FATHER'S FAVORITE QUOTE was "Prior preparation prevents poor performance." He liked it so much, he memorialized it inside the pantry door. Glancing at it daily as a child, I would roll my eyes, careful for him not to see, while thinking, "Seriously?"

As a military spouse, I've grown to appreciate this phrase as navigating this life is extremely challenging, and preparing for the small things makes the bigger challenges seem more manageable. Effective stress management isn't always linear or an exact science of repeated actions leading to the same results. It is the complicated product of honest self-assessment and good preparation.

At this point in our journey, you have successfully acquired much of the knowledge and skills needed to address stressful situations. You have debunked the complex nature of stress, reflected on the potential challenges you may face, self-assessed the significance of the common stressors associated with military life, and have a better game plan for each challenge you face through your response and management of stress. You now have the foundation to respond to these challenges at any time, even when you least expect them.

Unfortunately, even with the best intentions, things often do not go as planned. For military spouses, this couldn't be truer. Suppose your spouse is tagged with an out-of-cycle deployment. Going through the steps, you know this is an external source of stress imposed on you that is out of your control, and you understand this type of stress can be severe. Maybe you tried to alter your response by shifting negative initial thoughts of "this will be horrible" to more neutral ones such as, "this will be challenging, but I know I can do it." During this time, you might have purchased a journal and started writing down three things you were grateful for each night, only to find the stress remained. Despite your best intentions, things did not go as planned. You end up feeling frustrated and quickly losing hope that you can work through stressful situations successfully.

This is not a failure, but rather an opportunity to learn. "Prior preparation" is not just building knowledge and skills ahead of stressful situations, but also developing an ability to critically analyze past stressful events. Treat past stressful events as a form of investigation into both the event and yourself. Doing so cultivates learning opportunities for future stress.

Perseverance

Setbacks do not define you. Military life demands perseverance despite its many setbacks. Perseverance, or an ability to continue the course of action even in the face of difficult situations with little to no indication of success, is demonstrated over and over again by military spouses. For example, one month after moving into a new home, you find out your spouse's hours shift to lengthy night work with several intermittent TDYs. The boxes are still piled high against the wall, curtains and pictures await being hung, and you now face these tasks without your spouse being there. When you get the job done and use it to motivate you in other areas of your life, that is perseverance in action.

Perseverance becomes necessary to go beyond survival and truly thrive in stressful situations. Perseverance is not always easy, but there are specific techniques that can help you promote it in your life. Using these skills to maneuver through stressful situations may not solve all of your challenges, but it will allow you to continue moving forward and learn for the future.

Stress Inoculation

The term post-traumatic growth is becoming much more commonly used today. It comes from the work of two psychologists, David Feldman, PhD, and Lee Kravetz, MA, LMFT, who researched the phenomenon and found that in the wake of significant trauma, some individuals rebuild their lives, thrive, and grow in ways never previously imagined. These "super survivors" reflect the extraordinary ability to flourish after a personal tragedy, as opposed to struggle (post-traumatic stress disorder).

Surviving to Thriving

Phil, my husband of twenty-three years, was killed by someone he liked and trusted—someone he should have been able to trust because he wore a friendly uniform. Worse yet, the killer shot nine Americans in a room with over twenty other NATO Afghan troops, yet not one of them stood up or came to the defense of any of the men and one woman killed that day. In the immediate days after my husband had been assassinated, I couldn't get through five minutes without thinking of my devastating loss. This loss included more than the loss of my husband. It included the loss of faith in my country, my Air Force, my friendships, and myself. I fixated on the end and on the moments too awful to comprehend.

I could not sleep because of the intrusive thoughts that left me waking with tears and gasping for air. I isolated myself because I couldn't deal with the fear of figuring out life without Phil. I became a walking wounded woman who kept people at arm's length. I was afraid to feel. I consumed myself with work and with running. On the outside, I looked like I had it all together, but in every waking moment and nighttime dream, I was consumed with a yearning for what I did not have.

I began to fight to thrive versus survive. Instead of fleeing from my fears, I began to face them. My knees would shake and I would get physically sick, but each time, I accomplished even a small victory in standing up to my fear. I began to see possibilities where there were none before. It hasn't been easy, but I am living and not just surviving.

I made choices that many could not understand. I began running all over the world, and I took a job in first Germany and then Japan. I began to do public advocacy and to mentor other

trauma survivors because it allowed something positive to come
out of the worst moments of my life. Helping others became a way
to honor and remember Phil, who lost his life far too soon.

I liken the thrive versus survive journey to a marathon. I
have run more than 170 marathons. There is never one I haven't
wanted to quit. I know that I will feel worse tomorrow and the
next day, but I also know that if I look at only the step ahead, I
can get there. I may fall down. I may get lost. I may need a friend
to encourage me, but I can run the race if I focus only on the step
or moment in front of me.

Trauma is like that too. In the immediate aftermath, a person
survives one moment at a time. They cannot look too far ahead
because it is too overwhelming to the crushed soul. At a point
in the storm, a person will realize that the crushing moments
are not coming at the same frequency. It is at that point a choice
can be made—a choice to thrive rather than survive by looking
for opportunities and meaning or changing the loss these events
have brought. While a person cannot change the events or the
tragedies, they can choose the way forward. It is in that choice
that a person becomes a better person than they were before.
—Linda A., Air Force spouse

Thankfully, you do not need to experience a deep personal
tragedy like Linda's to be able to grow. As you already learned in
chapter one, any stressful situation, not necessarily a traumatic one,
can result in a positive, neutral, or negative experience. Stress can also
be a mixture of these effects. As a result, post-traumatic growth can
also be achieved when you walk away from a stressful situation with
a rewarding experience because you were able to rise to the occasion
and leave with a stronger version of yourself.

Unfortunately, many of the challenges associated with military
life leave us with an experience ranging somewhere between neutral
or negative. This is okay. These experiences provide the perfect
opportunity to learn and grow or acquire pre-traumatic stress growth.
Pre-traumatic stress growth, as opposed to post-traumatic growth,
is building up a social-emotional shield before the event, preparing

you for whatever lies ahead. By using smaller, less intense stressors as learning tools you can be better prepared for future big ones.

The military recognizes the importance of this concept and has adopted a version of pre-traumatic stress growth called stress inoculation. Stress inoculation, or building resistance to stress through exposure to stressful stimuli, requires three steps: (1) education, (2) skill acquisition, and (3) application and follow through. This process has proven effective in tactical jobs where demands are fast-paced and job tasks can be physically and psychologically intense. For example, United States Air Force Pararescuemen (PJs) and Combat Controllers (CCT) are required to recover downed or injured military personnel and direct military aircraft in hostile or denied regions. Similar to medical inoculation against diseases, these individuals are exposed to just enough stress to arouse defenses, but not enough that it overwhelms them. The most familiar is drown-proofing, where trainees have their feet and hands bound behind their back and get into a deep swimming pool. Then, they must swim from the bottom of the pool to the surface for breaths of air and perform a variety of maneuvers. Through this repetitive process of gradually exposing students to stress, they begin to recognize and understand their natural stress response and learn to control these responses when they emerge. In other words, by using a controlled, safe environment, they gradually build up a resistance or confidence to work through future real-life crises and high levels of stress in the water.

Pre-traumatic stress growth, as opposed to post-traumatic growth, is building up a social-emotional shield before the event, preparing you for whatever lies ahead.

Sound familiar? You have followed many of the same steps up to this point in the book by learning about stress and acquiring the skills needed to respond and manage your stress. Unlike military training, you do not need to create scenarios for stress growth. Allow the experiences associated with military life to be your teacher; your challenge is to be the student.

Critical Self-Analysis

If you hadn't been on a bike in five years, would you still remember how to ride? For most people, the answer is yes. This is due to what scientists call explicit and implicit learning. Explicit learning—what you are currently doing by reading this book— requires conscious observation, understanding, and memorization of content. Implicit learning often takes place without awareness or the intent to learn, and can involve a gradual accumulation of knowledge over time. Learning that begins as explicit may become implicit over time. Five years from now, after you learn the cycle of stress growth and successfully work through the cycle many times, it will become implicit for you. You may forget the stages of the cycle but you will continue to apply it in your life.

The final step before making the stress growth model an automatic part of your decision-making process is critical self-analysis. Think of this as an investigation, or as commonly referred to in the military, a hotwash of a recent stressful event. Similar to taking apart your child's toy to find out why it is not working, a critical analysis allows you to discover exactly how you operate under stress, increasing your preparedness for future stress. Be observant of the challenges you faced and debrief yourself once the situation is resolved. Ask yourself critical questions to understand what signs you noticed, how you responded, what you did well, and what you could have done better. A critical self-analysis can be applied to all situations, regardless of the positive, neutral, or negative end result. There is opportunity to learn in every situation.

Suppose you decide to enter a graduate program, one of your life-long goals established at a very young age. You go through the grueling application process and you are accepted, then you learn your spouse will deploy the first week of classes. Vacillating at first, you eventually decide your motivation for education outweighs the anticipatory fear of not being able to juggle all the demands on your time. You both begin your challenging journeys. After three months, you're exhausted and notice irritability with friends and family. Initial thoughts of "I don't think I can do this alone for six months" creep in, and you start to question whether to continue in the program.

You tell yourself to keep going, to push through, because you fear quitting will disappoint others, or even yourself. However, you know something must change. As an avid runner, you decide to double your biweekly runs to four times a week and start walking for thirty minutes on your off days to help alleviate some of your stress. You make it through the first semester, your spouse safely returns home, you've increased your fitness, and you're ecstatic! You rose to the occasion, although it was stressful at times, leaving you with a rewarding experience. Now analyze the situation and reflect on how you responded to stress.

Understand Your Stress Response

External vs Internal: In this situation there were two external stressors: graduate school and a deployment. There was also internal stress caused by your concern about additional demands on your time and your fear of disappointment.

Severity (frequency, duration, and intensity): The event contained both internal and external stress (increased frequency) across a six-month period (increased duration) and was managed with exercise (lower intensity) equaling moderate stress.

Effects (positive, neutral, negative, or combined): This was a positive experience as the goal was obtained by tackling stress through known coping skills.

Response (initial and following): Initially there were negative thoughts: "I don't think I can do this alone for six months." Most of the thoughts that followed were also negative and driven by fear of disappointment. Although positive behaviors resulted (management of stress through exercise), they were driven by negative thoughts. This could be a concern in the future. For example, this stressful event was moderate and if a future "critical" stressful event occurs, negative thoughts could dominate, take over, and lead to negative behaviors.

Management (physical, emotional, cognitive, behavioral): The stress was positively managed through known coping skills (exercise). Reflect on other techniques that could have been helpful too, such as journaling, social support, or meditation.

Self-Analysis:

"What signs did I notice?" (increased fatigue and irritability)

"How did I respond?" (negative thoughts of disappointment)

"What did I do well?" (managed stress with exercise)

"What could I have done better?" (change negative thoughts to more neutral or positive)

Increase Preparedness: In this example, the critical analysis lies within the follow-up response to stress. Negative internal thoughts remained after the initial response to learning about the deployment. Going forward, if after identifying initial negative response thoughts, you articulate neutral or positive alternatives and incorporate new thought patterns into the situation, you will be better prepared for future stress.

This critical analysis demonstrates that although the overall effect of this situation was positive, there was also still room to grow.

This same process can be applied to all experiences that result from a stressful situation. The more you practice analyzing a challenging situation in its entirety, the easier it becomes. It will help sharpen your skills needed to successfully overcome bigger challenges in the future. This process requires mental discipline and, much like skills presented earlier in this book, requires exposure and practice. It is a matter of paying attention, learning from the experience, and being curious and open to improve in the future.

Optimism, Hope, and Contentment

I remember as a child waking up on my grandmother's farm. I would wander into the kitchen, knowing my grandmother would be perched at the table playing solitaire with a hot cup of coffee. Starting at 4 a.m., she would play until she won, sometimes taking hours. I was fascinated by her morning ritual and finally asked one morning, "Why do you always play until you win?" She peered at me over her glasses and informed me, "We all have a choice in how we start our day, I choose to start every day with a win."

Adopting a mindset of "choosing to win" allows setbacks to shift from perceived losses to opportunities to win. Whether you are tackling a new project at work, connecting with friends in a new community, or learning new ways to cope with stress, overcoming doubt or fear is possible when you focus on what you can potentially gain out of the situation.

Realistic Optimism

Are you someone who sees the glass half empty or half full? An optimistic person, someone who generally sees the positive aspects in life rather than the negatives ones, would answer with an unwavering "half full!" This personality trait has been well understood through thousands of studies and shown to cause better resistance to depression during challenging events, better performance at work, and better physical health.

Pessimistic individuals, seeing the glass half empty, have a difficult time resisting the temptation to focus solely on the negative. The sensationalized negative news that inundates social media and television today is a common culprit for generating pessimism. As a society we often depend on these modes of communication for social connection and information sharing, which makes it increasingly difficult to avoid the negative news. However, if you hear negative messaging enough, you can start to believe it, taking a psychological toll in the form of depression, anxiety, or acute stress. Consider limiting your daily intake of these kinds of messages.

People are not hard wired as either optimistic or pessimistic. Every situation presents a new choice and perspective.

People are not hard wired as either optimistic or pessimistic. Every situation presents a new choice and perspective. Your challenge is to choose which side you want to fall on.

Pessimistic	Optimistic
Gives up easily	Never gives up
Fears taking the next step	Does not fear risk
Struggles to see the positive	Tries to see the positive
Easily disappointed	Not easily disappointed
Self-pity	Self-confidence
Problem seeker	Problem solver
Discouraging factor	Motivation factor
Destroys happiness	Gives happiness
Doubting	Hopeful

Optimism without concrete knowledge and skills can be just wishful thinking. Through all the challenges military spouses face, it is important to have realistic optimism. Realistic optimism is a mindset you develop through your experiences where you consider two different perspectives for each new stressful situation.

The first is having an awareness of, and appreciation for, the stress a particular experience poses and being honest about the challenges you are facing. You have achieved this, or are working toward this, by doing the work in this book. The second is knowing with complete certainty that your knowledge, skills, and judgment will arm you with the ability to minimize your stress and make the experience as positive as possible. Embracing future challenges with the new skills presented in this book serves as a foundation. Having a clear view of the stress and using the techniques in this book to create a future stress plan you are confident in is the core of realistic optimism.

Embracing optimism does not make us immune to stress and worry. However, adopting a balanced approach through knowledge and skills can build up resistance toward the temptation to focus

Milspouse Strength ~ Kendra Lowe

solely on the negative. Optimism can also teach us how to see what is going wrong and still be hopeful it will turn into a win.

Hope

Hope is an innate desire for things to change for the better. Generally, an optimistic person is more hopeful than others, but even the most pessimistic person can still find hope about something.

Hope is deeply rooted in life, whether you see it or not. We all hope for something: a better job, successful children, less stress. Hope helps define what we want in the future by envisioning it—perhaps hugging your spouse at the end of a deployment or seeing your children happy and healthy. It can make present challenges much easier to bear.

I can personally testify to the importance of hope. There are large chunks of time I do not remember during my freshman year at the Air Force Academy as my mind's self-protectiveness kicked in and created permanent blocks. But I can recall the visceral fear and suffocating depression that remained because of a vicious attack, impacting me enough that I still carry the label of PTSD today.

As I sat down with my psychologist and recounted my story again (post move), he stopped, and put down his paper and pencil. Looking at me rather intensely, he asserted that society's definition of PTSD is all wrong. It isn't a matter of post-traumatic stress disorder, but rather pre-thriving situational discomfort. He highlighted the fact that although I was not thriving at that moment, it was temporary. I was not completely broken. The fact that I was there, seeking help, meant I envisioned a future that did not include fear and overwhelming sadness.

In that moment something shifted, and a new sense of hope emerged. When I left his office on my final day working with him, I was still wearing the label of PTSD, but society's imposed scarlet letter had become a badge of honor—symbolizing the challenges I had overcome. I had hope.

Post-traumatic stress requires ongoing deliberate and intentional care. If you (or someone you care about) struggle with this type of stress, it may help to receive a reminder of your progress and that setbacks are temporary; reassurance that you have the ability to strengthen your body, mind, and spirit to protect from future stress; and encouragement to visualize a future in which you will thrive.

In addition to creating hopeful feelings by visualizing a positive outcome or desired future, reframing how you think of a current situation or ongoing challenge with post-traumatic stress can help you move forward in practical ways, much like when I adjusted my training after my knee injury.

In contrast to hope, hopelessness is an awful feeling that leaves you stuck. Shifting from hopelessness to hope starts with being open to the idea that a better outcome exists. Take the risk, there is more hope than you imagine. Thoughts associated with both positive and negative events can reflect a sense of hopelessness or hope.

Hopeless	Hopeful
"I'm lucky"	"I'm talented"
"I'm reckless."	"I made a bad choice."
"I can't find new friends."	"It may take time, but I know I am a good friend."
"This will never get easier."	"This too shall pass."

Especially in times of prolonged isolation, moving, deployments, or traumatic events, the advice to stay hopeful might make you roll your eyes. However, hope is more powerful than you might think for getting through life's challenges. Envisioning a better future can motivate future action. I often use the analogy of asking a group of people to sit around a table and share their most significant challenges. Each person at the table is shocked at what they hear, wondering how the others could get through such a big challenge. We have all been through challenges and found a way through; there is hope for your situation too. By analyzing stressful situations, you will see that you have overcome obstacles to get where you are today. They serve as markers in time of where you were then and where you are now. This creates another sense of hope—showing the progress you have made.

Contentment

Our brains are wired to seek pleasure over pain. When we feel good naturally, less resistance exists to the challenges we face. However, "I am happy" means something different for all of us. For some, being happy is a positive emotion associated with feelings: pleasure, warmth, thrills, comfort. These are momentary and involve little thinking. For others it could be associated with engagement: enjoying music, time with a friend, or being completely present and absorbed in your favorite book. Others define happiness by meaning in their lives or the desire to serve something bigger than themselves: military service, religion, politics, or family. Knowing these three types of contentment (feelings, engagement, meaning) is less important than knowing you can achieve happiness in different ways.

Shifting from hopelessness to hope starts with being open to the idea that a better outcome exists.

Depending on what happiness means to you, there may be more or less effective ways to increase happiness and joy in your life.

Increase Positive Feelings

Put into your life as many events as possible that produce positive emotions but consider spacing out the time between these events. For example, suppose you eat your favorite chicken marsala every night for two weeks. By the end of the two weeks, you will likely enjoy the dish far less than if you had eaten it once every week instead. Spacing out the time between pleasurable events allows you to maximize the return (positive effects) of those experiences.

Increase Positive Engagement

Try ways to savor or put conscious attention to positive engagement. If you just finished a meaningful book, one you didn't want to end, consider sharing it with friends. Including them in your experience increases your overall enjoyment of the experience. Another way is to anchor mental memories of an event. As you rock your child to sleep at night, feel the softness of the blanket, smell the lavender diffuser, listen to the soothing sound machine, and gently kiss the softness of your baby's head. Creating a sensory imprint of positive memories allows for quicker access to them and increases happiness as you re-experience those memories in the future.

Increase Positive Meaning

Increasing positive meaningful experiences is about aligning natural strengths with experiences. For example, you may notice that military spouses in your unit are struggling with a current deployment. Wanting to help but not knowing exactly how to start, you pull out your old bracelet stamping machine and start creating metal bracelets engraved with "be brave, be strong, be fearless." It becomes a symbol of strength for the deployment and you feel excited to be able to help. The combination of natural strength (creativity) with desire to help your friends (meaning) increased the overall positiveness of the experience.

We all want to feel happier. But avoid the cultural bias that says we are supposed to be happy all the time and when we are not something is wrong. Military life is full of challenges, upsets, and pain. It is reasonable to expect to not be happy sometimes. Feigning happiness represses our real feelings and experiences.

More Than a Pity Party

My husband was scheduled to deploy to Djibouti, Africa, on an early Monday morning. We had just spent a long weekend together preparing for an emotional goodbye, and we were both eager to "get it over with" so we could move on to the next challenge of the actual deployment. My husband always preferred private goodbyes at home, so I would hold it together until I saw his truck drive away. And then I would let myself feel everything for a week with a direct request for family and friends not to contact me.

Why, you may ask? Well, in the past, I would often be inundated with phone calls and text messages. My mom's: "Are you okay?" quickly followed by his mom, my dad, his brother, my sister, my best friend, his sister—you get the point. I grew tired of saying, "I'm okay," when it was a blatant lie but I knew if I verbalized that I was not okay, my front doorstep would soon be crowded with family members banging down the door, something I could not handle. … I asked myself what I could possibly do to alleviate my own stress during the pre-deployment phase. What I came up with was something that worked for me.

I told all family members and friends to not contact me for one week after he deployed. For one week, they were not allowed to reach out, to call, to check-in. I asked them to respect my wishes. This, I asserted, was what I needed to get through the transition. Essentially, I threw myself a solo, week-long pity party, but it worked. I was able to work through my feelings and begin the road to accepting my new normal. Make no mistake, it wasn't easy, as there were times during that week that I craved attention from family and friends, but overall, I knew it was what I needed. And, for the record, if my husband left on a Sunday at 8 a.m., then be assured all family members called, emailed, and checked in seven days later at 8 a.m., but by that point, I was ready. I was comfortable and prepared for my response whether it was "I'm okay," "I'm sad," or "I'm struggling." —Kate L., Army spouse

Contentment, or a general feeling of "okayness" with life, allows grace to accept what is and acknowledge what you are experiencing. Knowing it is okay to be down, depressed, anxious, or afraid sometimes is just as important as finding ways to increase your level of optimism, hope, or happiness.

You are now prepared for future challenges, equipped with the final skill: prior preparation. This critical self-analysis shifts your lens from reactionary to proactive by inviting you to clearly see opportunities to improve and grow. Proactive measures foster optimism, hope, and contentment because you have the ability to create more positive stress experiences.

You have gifted yourself control within a culture full of surprises, which is no easy feat. Embrace your gift by looking forward to future challenges, knowing military life is a perfect opportunity to put your new skills to the test!

Chapter Reflection

~ Note a time you persevered in military life. Was the result motivating, overwhelming, or simply a task you completed and left behind?

~ Have you or someone close to you experienced a traumatic event or been exposed to stress inoculation? What was the outcome? Why do you believe this was the case?

~ Work through a critical self-analysis of a current stressor. Identify the stress. Assess the severity, response to stress, or management of stress. Note areas for improvement.

~ After completing the critical self-analysis, note the main ways you intend to prepare for future stress.

~ Do you believe you tend toward more optimistic or pessimistic responses to challenges? What can you do to look at situations more optimistically? Review "realistic optimism." How will you start your day with a "win?"

~ What currently brings you hope? What are your hopes for the future? Envision what your ideal life looks like and create a plan for how you will build that life.

~ Do you feel happy through feelings, engagement, or meaning in life? How can you increase these experiences? Be specific.

~ What are some of the most significant tools you now have for understanding and responding to stress? How will you incorporate them into your life? Discuss your thoughts about your new stress growth model with your spouse, trusted friend, or support group.

Afterword

~~~~~~~~~~~~~~~~~~~~~~~~~~~~~

I BEGAN THIS BOOK WITH A STORY about traveling overseas, so I will end with our trip back to the United States.

We prepared for months prior to our actual departure date, gathering school records, dog records, and medical records; scheduling the move; cleaning and purging; and saying our final goodbyes—the list was endless and challenging. I knew I didn't want a repeat of the severe stress I felt in the first few months on the island.

Three months out we were presented with our first big challenge. Our dog could not weigh more than 99.9 pounds combined weight with the dog crate. Welp! Our dog needed to lose eighteen pounds in order to fly. As I was in the middle of writing my book, I saw this as another opportunity to reflect on what I had learned. I tested myself to see if I had actually changed my lens on stress. I acknowledged that this stressor was out of my control and rationalized that we had time to implement a plan: walk him three times a day and slowly cut back on food. I told myself it would be okay.

One month out presented the next challenge as the onslaught of goodbyes began with colleagues, friends, and those we now considered family. We all felt it, so much so that my five-year-old son started to wet the bed. It was yet another opportunity to pull out some tools. We started to journal, writing down our favorite moments in Okinawa. The kids printed pictures to give to friends, and my eldest started deep breathing before bed. The rollercoaster of emotions was still there but it was managed with contentment of what we were feeling, hope of seeing family members soon, and optimism for our next adventure.

One week out, we stuffed our family of five and golden retriever into a one room temporary living facility as it was the only pet-friendly room available. We laughed at our newfound appreciation for the phrase "living on top of each other." Rationalizing the situation again, we told ourselves this was only temporary.

Finally, we entered the airport, feeling as though we had conquered this test, only to be met by yet another challenge. The Japanese ticket agent informed us that our dog could not fly. Not because of his weight, but because we did not have an approved mat on the bottom of his crate. Here was yet another opportunity for growth. Instead of being angry or frustrated that this requirement was certainly not on the twenty-page document they provided three months ago, I took a deep breath, and thought of a potential solution. I turned to my suitcase and began digging for anything that resembled a mat. My pajamas happened to fit perfectly.

Reflecting back, the challenges on our move back to the United States created opportunities to put my knowledge and skills in action and to see what I was capable of. This certainly will not be my last challenge with military life, but I know I am capable of "wins."

You too now have the knowledge and skills needed to understand stress, self-assess the severity, control your response, and manage stress—leaving you better prepared for future challenges. But your journey does not end here. Continue to evaluate the lens through which you see stress with the tools you have gained throughout this book. Continue to take risks by seeking moments to learn, adjust, and pivot. Continue to be open to improving yourself and your relationships with others. In a few years, look back and think about how far you have come. In doing so, your challenges will morph into opportunities to grow, adapt, and celebrate wins.

Life challenges us all to make deliberate choices every day, not least of which are the powerful choices of who you are and who you will become. Embrace your newly created mantra: every challenge is an opportunity.

Resources

~~~~~~~~~~~~~~~~~~~~~~~~~~~~~~~

For readers who want to learn more about the concepts presented in this book, I share the following resources, based on years of research, education, and mentorship.

Chapter 1 ~ Understand

"Impact of Military Deployment on Family Relationships." Kendra N. Lowe, Katharine S. Adams, Blaine L. Browne, and Kerry T. Hinkle, 2012. *Journal of Family Studies.*

"5 Ways to Manage Military Spouse Stress." Kendra Lowe, 2016. *Military Spouse.*

"Medical Definition of Stress." William C. Shiel Jr., 2018. Retrieved from http://www.medicinenet.com/stress/definition.htm.

"Cortisol: Why the 'Stress Hormone' Is Public Enemy No. 1." Christopher Bergland, 2013. *Psychology Today.*

"Stress Effects on the Body." American Psychological Association, 2018. http://www.apa.org/topics/stress/body.

"Stress-Related Growth: Building a More Resilient Brain." Anna S. Ord, Kathryn R. Stranahan, Robin A. Hurley, and Katherine H. Taber, 2020. *The Journal of Neuropsychiatry and Clinical Neurosciences.*

"Best Practices for Stress Measurement: How to measure psychological stress in health research." Alexandra D. Crosswell and Kimberly G. Lockwood, 2020. *Health Psychology Open.*

"Changes in Appearance in the Presence of Major Stress Events." Megan E. Stitz and John D. Pierce Jr., 2013. *SAGE Open.*

"Stress sensitivity and stress sensitization in psychopathology: An introduction to the special section." Kate L. Harkness, Elizabeth P. Hayden, and Nestor L. Lopez-Duran, 2015. *Journal of Abnormal Psychology.*

The Prevention of Anxiety and Depression: Theory, Research, and Practice. David J. A. Dozois, and Keith S. Dobson, 2004. American Psychological Association.

Clinical Practice Guidelines for the Treatment of Posttraumatic Stress Disorder (PTSD) in Adults, 2017. American Psychological Association.

Chapter 2 ~ Self-Assess

"Military Children from Birth to Five Years." Joy D. Osofsky and Molinda M. Chartrand, 2013. *Future of Children.*

Combat Stress Reaction: The Enduring Toll of War. Zahava Solomon, 1993. Springer.

"Military Children and Families: Strengths and Weaknesses During Peace and War." Nansook Park, 2011. *American Psychologist.*

"Welcoming Them Home: Supporting Service Members and Their Families in Navigating the Tasks of Reintegration." Ursula B. Bowling and Michelle D. Sherman, 2008. *Professional Psychology: Research and Practice.*

"Deployment: An Overview." Military.com, 2014. Retrieved from http://www.military.com/deployment/deployment-overview.html.

"The Social Adjustment Rating Scale." Thomas Holmes and Richard Rahe, 1967. *Journal of Psychosomatic Research.*

"Defense Primer: Exceptional Family Member Program (EFMP)." Congressional Research Service, 2020. Retrieved from http://sgp.fas.org/crs/natsec/ IF11049.pdf.

"EFMP/Special Needs." Military One Source, 2019. Retrieved from http://www.militaryonesource.mil/family-relationships/special-needs/ exceptional-family-member/.

"EFMP is Positive for Families Not Negative for Careers." Nikki Maxwel, 2013. US Army. Retrieved from http://www.army.mil/article/110436/EFMP_is_ positive_not_negative_for_careers/.

"A Call to Duty: Educational Policy and School Reform Addressing the Needs of Children from Military Families." Monica Christina Esqueda, Ron Avi Astor, and Kris M. Tunac De Pedro, 2012. *Educational Researcher.*

"The Effect of Geographic Moves on Mental Healthcare Utilization of Children." Jeffrey Millegan, Robert McLay, and Charles Engel, 2014. *Journal of Adolescent Health.*

"Month of the Military Child." Department of Defense, 2017. Retrieved from http://dod.defense.gov/News/Special-Reports/0417_militarychild/.

"The Short-Term Stress Response - Mother Nature's Mechanism for Enhancing Protection and Performance Under Condition of Threat, Challenge, and Opportunity." Firdaus S. Dhabhar, 2019. *Frontiers In Neuroendocrinology.*

"2018 Military Family Lifestyle Survey: Findings and Analysis." Hisako Sonethavilay, Rosalinda V. Maury, Jennifer L. Hurwitz, Rachel Linsner Uveges, Jennifer L. Akin, Jamie Lynn De Coster, and Jessica D. Strong, 2018. Blue Star Families Department of Research and Policy. Retrieved from http://bluestarfam.org/wp-content/uploads/2019/03/2018MFLS-ComprehensiveReport-DIGITAL-FINAL.pdf.

"The Emotional Cycles of Deployment: A Military Family Perspective." Simon H. Pincus, Robert House, Joseph Christenson, and Lawrence E. Adler, 2001. *US Army Medical Department Journal.*

"Combat Duty in Iraq and Afghanistan, Mental Health Problems, and Barriers to Care." Charles W. Hoge, Carl A. Castro, Stephen C. Messer, Dennis McGurk, Dave I. Cotting, and Robert L. Koffman, 2004. *New England Journal of Medicine.*

Chapter 3 ~ Respond

You and Your Emotions. Maxie C. Maultsby Jr. and Allie Hendricks, 1974. Psychiatry Outpatient Clinic, University of Kentucky Medical Center.

Rational Behavioral Therapy. Maxie C. Maultsby Jr., 1990. Rational Self-Help Aids.

The Mind and the Brain: Neuroplasticity and the Power of Mental Force. Jeffrey M. Schwartz and Sharon Begley, 2003. Harper Perennial.

"The Brief Resilience Scale: Assessing the Ability to Bounce Back." Bruce W. Smith, Jeanne Dalen, Kathryn Wiggins, Erin Tooley, Paulette Christopher, and Jennifer Bernard, 2008. *International Journal of Behavioral Medicine.*

Mental Mechanisms: Philosophical Perspectives on Cognitive Neuroscience. William Bechtel, 2008. Psychology Press.

"The Road to Resilience." American Psychological Association, 2011. Retrieved from http://www.apaservices.org/practice/good-practice/building-resilience.pdf.

"Effects of self-verbalizations upon emotional arousal and performance: a test of rational-emotive theory." Gregory Bonadies and Barry Bass, 1984. *Perceptual and Motor Skills.*

"Role of irrational beliefs in depression and anxiety: a review." K. Robert Bridges and Richard J. Harnish, 2010. *Health.*

"Rational and irrational beliefs and psychopathology." Christopher M. Browne, E. Thomas Dowd, and Arthur Freeman. In *Rational and Irrational Beliefs in Human Functioning and Disturbances: Implications for Research, Theory, and Practice,* eds. Daniel David, Steven Lynn, and Albert Ellis, 2010. Oxford University Press.

"Rational and irrational beliefs in primary prevention in mental health." Donald A. Caserta, E. Thomas Dowd, Daniel David, and Albert Ellis. In *Rational and Irrational Beliefs in Human Functioning and Disturbances: Implications for Research, Theory, and Practice,* eds. Daniel David, Steven Lynn, and Albert Ellis, 2010. Oxford University Press.

"Rational psychotherapy and individual psychology." Albert Ellis, 1957. *Journal of Individual Psychology.*

"On the origin and development of rational-emotive theory." Albert Ellis, 1987. In *Key Cases in Psychotherapy*, ed. Windy Dryden. New York University Press.

Chapter 4 ~ Manage

"The Women of Sparta: Athletic, Educated, and Outspoken Radicals of the Greek World." 2017. *Ancient History Encyclopedia*.

"Research: Why Breathing is so Effective at Reducing Stress." Emma Seppälä, Christina Bradley, and Michael R. Goldstein, 2020. *Harvard Business Review*.

"Relaxation Techniques: What You Need To Know." National Center for Complementary and Integrative Health, 2021. Retrieved from http://www.nccih.nih.gov/health/relaxation-techniques-what-you-need-to-know.

"Progressive muscle relaxation: a remarkable tool for therapists and patients." Peter A. Mackereth and Lynne Tomlinson. In *Integrative Hypnotherapy*, eds. Anne Cawthorn and Peter A. Mackereth, 2010. Churchill Livingstone.

"Nature-Based Guided Imagery as an Intervention for State Anxiety." Jessica Nguyen and Eric Brymer, 2018. *Frontiers in Psychology*.

Advances in ABC Relaxation: Applications and Inventories. Jonathan C. Smith, editor, 2001. Springer.

"Effects of Physical Exercise on Cognitive Functioning and Wellbeing: Biological and Psychological Benefits." Laura Mandolesi, Arianna Polverino, Simone Montuori, Francesca Foti, Giampaolo Ferraioli, Pierpaolo Sorrentino, and Giuseppe Sorrentino, 2018. *Frontiers in Psychology*.

"A prototype analysis of gratitude: varieties of gratitude experiences." Nathaniel M. Lambert, Steven M. Graham, and Frank D. Fincham, 2009. *Personal and Social Psychology Bulletin*.

"Gratitude, like other positive emotions, broadens and builds." Barbara L. Fredrickson. In *The Psychology of Gratitude*, eds. Robert A. Emmons and Michael E. McCullough, 2004. Oxford University Press.

"Gratitude influences sleep through the mechanism of pre-sleep cognitions." Alex M. Wood, Stephen Josep, Joanna Lloyd, and Samuel Atkins, 2009. *Journal of Psychosomatic Research*.

"Effects of gratitude on subjective well-being, self-construal, and memory." Ozge Gurel Kirgiz, 2008. *Dissertation Abstracts International*.

Sensory Integration and the Unity of Consciousness, eds. David Bennett and Christopher Hill, 2014. MIT Press.

"Recommended amount of sleep for a healthy adult: a joint consensus statement of the American Academy of Sleep Medicine and Sleep Research Society." Nathaniel F. Watson, M. Sefwan Badr, Gregory Belenky, et al., 2015. *Sleep*.

"Pathways Leading to Successful Coping and Health." Aaron Antonovsky. In *Learned Resourcefulness: On Coping Skills, Self-Control, and Adaptive Behavior*, ed. M. Rosenbaum, 1990. Springer-Verlag.

"Preservation of the Force and Family." United States Special Operations Command (USSOCOM), 2019. Retrieved from http://www.socom.mil/POTFF.

"Building Communities of Care for Military Families and Children." Harold Kudler and Rebecca I. Porter, 2013. *The Future of Children*.

"Engaging Military Parents in a Home-Based Reintegration Program: A Consideration of Strategies." Abigail M. Ross and Ellen R. DeVoe, 2014. *Health and Social Work*.

Overcoming Procrastination. Albert Ellis and William J. Knaus, 1977. Institute for Rational Living

Chapter 5 ~ Grow

Clinical Practice Guidelines for the Treatment of Posttraumatic Stress Disorder (PTSD) in Adults. American Psychological Association, 2017. Retrieved from http://www.apa.org/ptsd-guideline/ptsd.pdf.

"2014 Military Family Lifestyle Survey: Findings and Analysis." Deborah A. Bradbard, Rosalinda V. Maury, Michele Kimball, Jennifer C.M. Wright, Cammy Elquist LoRé, Kathleen Levingston, Cristin Shiffer, Gail Simon-Boyd, Jennifer A. Taylor, and AnnaMaria Mannino White, 2014. Blue Star Families Department of Research and Policy. Retrieved from http://surface.syr.edu/ivmf/56.

"Stress Contagion: Physiological Covariation Between Mothers and Infants." Sara F. Waters, Tessa V. West, and Wendy Berry Mendes, 2014. *Psychological Science*.

"The relationship between the big five personality factors and burnout: a study among volunteer counselors." Arnold B. Bakker, Karen I. Van der Zee, Kerry A. Lewig, and Maureen F. Dollard, 2006. *The Journal of Social Psychology*.

"Time bandits: how they are created, why they are tolerated, and what can be done about them." David J. Ketchen Jr., Christopher W. Craighead, and M. Ronald Buckley, 2008. *Business Horizons*.

Stress Inoculation Training: A preventative and treatment approach. Donald Meichenbaum, 1985. Pergamon Press.

"The effects of stress inoculation training for first year law students." Richard Sheehy and John J. Horan, 2004. *International Journal of Stress Management*.

Supersurvivors: The Surprising Link Between Suffering and Success. David B. Feldman and Lee Daniel Kravetz, 2015. Harper Wave Publishing.

How to Survive Unbearable Stress. Steven L. Burns, 1990. International Medical Press.

The Backbone of Our Military: Perceptions and Experiences from Modern Military Spouses. United Services Organization (USO), 2018. Retrieved from http://www.marvinstrategies.com/our-work.

Airman and Family Resilience: Lessons from the Scientific Literature. Sarah O. Meadows, Laura L. Miller, and Sean Robson, 2015. RAND Corporation. Retrieved from http://www.rand.org/pubs/research_reports/RR106.html.

The Psychological Needs of US Military Service Members and Their Families: A Preliminary Report. American Psychological Association Presidential Task Force on Military Deployment Services for Youth, Families, and Service Members, 2007. Retrieved from http://www.apa.org/about/policy/military-deployment-services.pdf.

"Great expectations: A meta-analytic examination of optimism and hope." Gene M. Alarcon, Nathan A. Bowling, and Steven Khazon, 2013. *Personality and Individual Differences.*

"The role of hope in psychotherapy." J. Frank, 1968. *International Journal of Psychiatry.*

"Development of the Contentment with Life Assessment Scale (CLAS): Using Daily Life Experiences to Verify Levels of Self-Reported Life Satisfaction." Loraine F. Lavallee, P. Maurine Hatch, Alex C. Michalos, and Tara McKinley, 2007. *Social Indicators Research.*

"Costs and benefits of realism and optimism." Lisa Bortolotti and Magdalena Antrobus, 2015. *Current Opinion in Psychiatry.*

"The future of optimism." Christopher Peterson, 2000. *American Psychologist.*

Acknowledgments

~~~~~~~~~~~~~~~~~~~~~~~~~~~~~~~~

OUR MILITARY SERVICE MEN AND WOMEN fight for our country because they have been called to be part of something greater than themselves, and in so doing have asked their families to do the same. It is often the families behind the service men and women that are asked to put aside their personal comforts and desires so that our nation can continue to be the strongest global power. Thank you to all these families for sacrificing for our nation, for standing behind our military men and women so it is possible for them to put the mission first, and for providing the strength and stability for the family.

To my family and friends who have listened, encouraged, and mentored me every step along the way. You have proven that it truly takes a village.

I'm eternally grateful to Karen Pavlicin and the Elva Resa team who saw potential and pushed me beyond my comfort zone. Your talent and compassion allows everyone you touch to be the best version of themselves.